THE JOYS OF EVERYDAY Ritual

THE JOYS OF EVERYDAY Ritual

Spiritual Recipes to Celebrate Milestones, Ease Transitions, and Make Every Day Sacred

BARBARA BIZIOU

ST. MARTIN'S GRIFFIN
NEW YORK

Cover and interior art by Lynda Montgomery

Designed by Susi Oberhelman

www.stmartins.com

ISBN 0-312-28435-7

First published in the United States by Golden Books Publishing Co., Inc., as
The Joy of Ritual

First St. Martin's Griffin Edition: November 2001

10 9 8 7 6 5 4 3 2 1

To the memory of my sister, Sandi Winer,
and to my father, Julius Winer.

May they both rest in The Divine Presence.

Contents

BECOMING THE RITUAL LADY

"SO *YOU'RE THE RITUAL LADY*— what got you into this?"

"Do you do pagan rites?"

"Are you a witch?"

People often ask me these questions when they hear that I hold workshops on rituals. I can tell from the sometimes amazed, often skeptical looks in their eyes that, to some, the word *ritual* evokes a vision of frenzied, naked savages beating tom-toms as they dance around a blazing fire; others picture me performing some kind of secretive hocus-pocus. For many, a ritual suggests magic—something otherworldly, sacrilegious, and maybe even evil. Some people associate rituals with religious rites they were forced to do as children—and dreaded.

In all fairness, not everyone has a cynical reaction. Often, adults fondly remember annual Easter egg hunts, Christmas-tree-decorating parties, Chanukkah candle-lighting ceremonies, or songs and chants that recurred with each religious holiday. Still, most people believe that rituals are esoteric and imposing and that they must be performed by a cler-gyman or a spiritual master; they don't think that *they* can perform rituals. And they certainly don't see how rituals can be part of their everyday lives.

If you're picking up this book, you, too, are probably curious, suspicious, or harboring certain negative associations related to ritual. If so, read on. You're not alone. Many people who sign up for my workshops arrive with misperceptions about what rituals are and why they can enhance our lives.

A TURNING POINT

It took me awhile to acknowledge my inner power, let alone grasp the idea that I could enhance it through the use of ritual. As a child, even as a young adult, I went with the flow, first conforming to my family's customs, then joyfully adopting those of my peers. I came of age in the sixties and embraced the counterculture with a vengeance. There I was, all tie-dye and velvet, decked out in love beads, wanting to spread love and change the world. After college I traveled, lived in many countries, and in Italy I even landed a role in the movie *Barbarella*. Outwardly I appeared eccentric, to the envy of some of my more staid sorority sisters who wrote to me from home, but inside I still felt like an innocent little girl. Before I knew it, my adventures drew to a close. My roots outweighed my carefree image and there I was, married, living in California, and a mother-to-be.

In July of 1971, twenty-six years old and three months pregnant, I returned to New York for a family emergency. Sandi, my twenty-four-year-old sister, was dying of brain cancer. Diagnosed a month before my wedding in 1969, it now looked like the end was near. Although her illness had shaken our family for two years, none of us would acknowledge that she was dying until that moment. In those days, *no one* talked about death, and *cancer* was a word we only whispered. I tried to work up the nerve to talk to Sandi, but when I finally did, it was too late. In fact, my brother said that she wanted to tell me something important, but by the time I arrived in New York her speech was failing, as well as her memory. She spoke but her words made no sense. To this day, I'll never know what she wanted to say or if she understood anything that I said to her.

When Sandi died, my family and I again went through the motions. As we all said Kaddish, the prayer for the dead, I felt as if the words had no real meaning. But during the traditional funeral service, I felt Sandi's presence so strongly that I was startled and looked up. I saw her standing there, only a few feet away. I wasn't sure if she was real or imagined, but it was a great comfort to me at the time. Still, I never fully grieved for my sister. After the funeral, we all went back to our family home and sat shiva, the week-long mourning period. But for some reason I couldn't seem to cry—not for the unspoken words I had longed for her to speak, nor for all of the conversations we would never have.

In fact, everyone warned me not to mourn her too deeply. "It will harm your baby," they told me. I believed them because a part of me was so afraid of grieving that I probably felt relieved not to have to participate in the process. Looking back at that time, I realize that I was so closed off it was as if I never even attended the funeral.

I also had the disconcerting sense that Sandi had been reincarnated as my son, Jourdan, who was born six months after she died. By then I had begun to read about altered states of consciousness and Eastern spirituality. I heard people talk about cycles of birth and death—how a grandmother dies and then a child is born to carry on the chain of life. Because Sandi's death and Jourdan's birth occurred so closely together, I thought that maybe, somehow, he *was* her. I shared my anxiety with no one—I just pushed the feelings away in a neat package of uneasiness wrapped in grief and tried to ignore them.

Often, that which we try hardest to avoid becomes our greatest teacher, our most precious gift. Not surprisingly, Sandi's death proved to be mine, but it was some twenty years in coming.

MY TWO SELVES

As my generation segued into the self-centered seventies, love-ins gave way to consciousness-raising—changing the world became less important than changing ourselves. The process hinged upon shifting definitions and expectations, especially those involving gender roles. In such a state of cultural flux, marriages fell apart, including mine. I was thirty-two, Jourdan was five, and for the first time in my life I not only needed to "find" myself, but I also had to figure out a way to support the two of us. I left California for New York, as much to seek my fortune as to reconnect with family and friends. I hoped to satisfy the increasingly intense longing for something deeper in my life.

With a multitude of other baby boomers, I had begun to explore various aspects of the Human Potential Movement—a community of seekers immersed in a mix of non-Freudian psychotherapies, feminist philosophy, Eastern religions, and different schools of yoga and meditation. Two of my most important spiritual mentors were Omraam Mikhaël Aïvanhov, the Bulgarian master who

taught surya yoga, and Hilda Charlton, an American who spent eighteen years in India studying with many holy men and women, including the highly respected Sai Baba. Through their teachings, I learned to meditate, connect to my spirit guides, and receive clear direction about my purpose in this lifetime. I also mastered many healing techniques that became the foundation for much of my later work. Robert Fritz, the founder of the Institute for Human Evolution, opened the door to the creative process with his course, "Technologies for Creating," which I first learned as his student and then taught as an instructor. For many years, I also privately coached people from all walks of life to generate their visions and manifest change in their lives.

From each of my teachers, I found something that struck a personal chord. And I recognized a common theme: In everything there is Spirit that connects us to the greater forces in the universe. We are all a part of this Spirit and it is a part of each of us. I realized that I was beginning to unearth that deeper "something" I once yearned to find.

But I got more than I bargained for, because when I started practicing meditation, I began to see Sandi. No longer able to keep her at bay, I experienced tremendous sadness and pain. The more open I was to her presence, the more she was with me. In my dreams and in my free-form writing, the visions and messages were incredibly clear. Often, at night when I was the most quiet, I'd sense her nearby. Sometimes, it was as if she were actually talking to me. (Years later, my son told me that beginning around the age of three, he, too, saw her face. He remembers playing with his toys or drawing and suddenly feeling something in the room—a gentle, loving presence. Out of the corner of his eye, he would see the face of a woman. It gave him comfort.)

As time went on, I not only started to relax during these experiences, but also to welcome them. However, in the beginning meditation was difficult for me—twenty minutes seemed like an awfully long time to sit still. Yet with practice and the realization that I was, indeed, tapping into a mysterious, powerful, and loving universal force, "sitting" became less of a discipline and more of a joyous experience.

By the mid-eighties, I was considered a master teacher of empowerment, able to help others connect to their dreams and give them the tools to make them happen. People began to ask for private consultations, yet I never thought of my growing practice as my "real work." In fact, my life was a bit schizophrenic. Earning my living first in the fashion industry and later in television, I lived out other people's expectations, patterning my professional self on the only role models I knew—my father and other high-achieving men who focused primarily on business. Though I was a success by all the standard measures—salary, position, the regard of my coworkers—I felt like I lived simultaneously in two very different realms. In one, I was constantly striving to *achieve*, always running somewhere and accomplishing something. In the other, I strove to discover who I was as a woman, mother, teacher, friend, daughter, and even businesswoman, by doing just the opposite—trying to slow down and spending more time in meditation and prayer.

"Being is lost in becoming," warned the master Sai Baba, as though describing my life at that point. My true passion—the place where I felt internally connected—was satisfied in the courses I conducted and the personal counseling I offered. Through these pursuits, I was finding a connection to my inner self *and* to something greater.

But while I was beginning to gain a sense of what being "whole" was all about—an integration of mind, body, and soul—I didn't know how to bring my spiritual self into my work or, more important, how to modify my work to have a spiritual focus. And I worried, if I left the world of commerce, would I be able to pay my bills? Would my family think I was crazy for wanting to "just teach those workshops," as my father had once suggested? What kind of role model would I be for my son? The awful confusion of it all drove me to feel like a failure and a charlatan. There I was, a business "superwoman" by day and "priestess" by night, running workshops on empowerment and success on weeknights and weekends—but I couldn't figure out how to make *my* life mesh.

LISTENING TO GRAINS OF SAND

So, you might ask, what does all of this have to do with rituals? I didn't realize it at the time but I had already begun making rituals a part of my life: In addition to Jewish holidays, I also celebrated some Christian holidays with Jourdan since his father is Christian. By this point I was meditating every morning, which helped me plan my day; I lit candles and used aromatherapy when I wanted to calm myself; I took baths whenever I needed to "loosen up."

Every Tuesday night at my New York apartment, I hosted a group where regulars and assorted guests came together to meditate and send our combined energy out to the world. During part of the evening we formed a "healing circle." One by one, each person called out a name, and we as a group visualized a glowing ball of white light—symbolic of healing—and concentrated on directing our thoughts and collective energy to help that person. Many of us had parents who were getting frail and some of us had friends with AIDS,

so our healing circle was always a powerful, comforting ceremony. These experiences were far from the prescribed, rote rituals of my childhood in that they were personally structured and intentioned. And although I felt very connected to them, I still didn't identify them as *rituals*.

By the late eighties that began to change. I had been initiated into the practice of Johrei, an Eastern spiritual organization. A large part of Johrei centered on rituals of appreciation, purification, and healing. I learned how to draw a godlike healing energy from the universe—what some would call a laying-on of hands—and after many years of practice, I was honored with a sacred scroll dedicated to my home. Written in Japanese calligraphy, it said "Great bright light of the supreme God." I could feel the power of the words purging my apartment of negative energy. Johrei became part of my own daily practice. I created an altar in my apartment where I said my morning prayers and took time to appreciate all of my blessings. I began to channel Johrei to others—sending divine light to their Spirit.

When did I realize that I was on a path to becoming "the ritual lady"? Very slowly, over time. Like most people, I don't receive great insights delivered like a thunderbolt à la Charlton Heston's revelation in *The Ten Commandments*. Instead, answers and guidance are meted out to me in small bits, one at a time, like tiny grains of sand. If I listen carefully to my dreams, and to the thoughts that come into my head during prayer and meditation, I receive a tiny particle of knowledge that I put on a shelf in my mind. Eventually I notice that a fairly big mound of sand has accumulated on the shelf.

Such a mound had piled up by 1994, when I went to Prescott, Arizona, to participate in a two-week spiritual retreat with W. Brugh Joy, M.D., a physician who teaches workshops on the mind-body-spirit connection as well as the connections between Eastern and Western thought. Perhaps because of the work I had been doing on my own, and Brugh's focus on integrating these important dichotomies, I was ready to carefully examine the collected grains of sand.

Several important changes became apparent to me as I moved through the series of individual and group exercises Brugh had planned for us. I felt a richness in the extended silences and a power in the collective and individual rituals that we created. This was the first time I experienced being in silence for more than a few hours. My senses grew more attuned and refined; I *saw* colors, *listened* to sounds, and *smelled* the fragrances around me. After the second day of fasting and silence, my intuition sharpened; I could sense the feelings of others and hear the wisdom of my spirit guides. I finally understood

that it was time to complete a ritual of my own—to say good-bye to Sandi and grieve her death.

On the seventh day, during a three-day period of silence and fasting, I left the group and made my way into the sparse Arizona landscape. I walked in silent meditation until I spotted a beautiful tree. I dug a hole near the tree so that I could literally pour my grief—my tears—into it. In such an open-hearted space, vulnerable and free to express my emotions, I felt comfortable talking to Sandi. I told her how much I missed her, how sorry I was that I hadn't really said good-bye, and how I longed for the living relationship that her death cut short. The more I talked, the harder I cried. I rocked myself—I knew from reading about the rituals of other cultures that this movement could also help me access my grief. I talked and cried and the tears poured into that hole. At one point, it started to rain and I felt God's acknowledgment of my ritual. (Years later, I discovered that the Balinese believe that God has heard your prayers if it rains after a sacred ceremony.)

I was covered in mud when I returned to my room. I took a shower and went swimming to symbolize my wish for purification—my intention was to leave behind all of the pain and grief. I now understood the custom of washing one's hands when leaving a Jewish cemetery. Afterward, I dressed in white to express my sense of purity, anointed myself with my favorite jasmine oil, which signifies love, and wrote down all of the commitments I wanted to make to myself. I felt different—new, lighter, less burdened.

It may sound contrived, but the experiences at that retreat—specifically, the conscious act of creating my first ritual—initiated me into a new phase of my life. The once-constant chatter in my mind became a whisper. I felt a sudden sense of freedom as I realized that my spiritual progress no longer depended on the approval of others. Instead of setting goals because I wanted something, or thought it would be good for me, I moved into a "heart-centered" space—following my *feelings*, rather than my head. My orientation turned from *doing* and *manipulating* to *allowing* Spirit to live through me. I began to listen to the inner voice that guided me. And, for the first time in my life, I had a sense of how I fit into the larger scheme of things.

BECOMING THE "RITUAL LADY"

Returning from Brugh's retreat, I saw the world with new eyes. I recognized the rituals that I was already doing unconsciously before going to Arizona. I began to create rituals with the purpose of transforming everyday events into sacred moments. My morning shower became a purifi-cation ritual. Before a meal, I blessed the food that I ate. I took time to give thanks for all I had.

I began to see that when I gave conscious thought and positive energy, I received positive energy in return. Thus, through my rituals I symbolically planted seeds of appreciation for my life and then watched them sprout. Even the simplest rituals empowered me, calmed me, and brought new vitality and richness into mundane routines.

I studied the rituals of ancient civilizations and modern-day societies. I reviewed the different cultures I had encountered in my adult life and understood how important and pervasive rituals were for those societies. When I was in Israel, high atop Masada, a mountain nearly impossible to climb, I recalled seeing a *mikva*, a ritual bath. In Italy, among ruins and archaeological digs, I had seen artifacts and wall drawings that depicted rituals of girls' initiation into adulthood. Suddenly, my eyes were open to meanings that I had previously overlooked.

My intense curiosity led me to participate in various rites and rituals—a Native American ceremony for the full moon, a Chinese new year celebration, a Scandinavian tribute to Santa Lucia, a Buddhist empowerment rite. I realized that even though my parents didn't practice the lighting of Shabbat candles, I had adapted a version of that ancient Jewish ritual when I lit candles during my own prayers and meditation.

I explored and expanded my repertoire. I experimented further, creating specific rituals to help release old, limiting beliefs and adopt new ones, and to deal with stress, fears, and, perhaps most important, guide me through tough transitions. Soon, I began to share my rituals with others and create new ones for my son, family, and friends. In my own life and in theirs, I saw that adding the sacred was a prime ingredient for leading a joyful, meaningful existence. The acknowledgment of a force greater than ourselves—whether we call it God, Goddess, or Higher Power—lets us know that we're never alone or without guidance. So simple, but easily overlooked in the fast pace of life.

The next natural phase was to incorporate rituals into my empowerment workshops mentioned earlier—a step I contemplated with a great deal of trepidation. I decided to add a ritual of release to my "Women and Success" workshop, which I had cocreated and run for six years with career counselor Allie Roth. But I wondered how the enrollees—high-powered executive women accustomed to seminars with flip charts and simple sharing—would react to my "coming out" as a kind of priestess.

At my next workshop, I played a recording of Native American drums in the background to help move the participants into a ritual space within their hearts. The room was dead quiet, except for the music. I gave each woman a slip of paper to write down all of the people, feelings, and fears that no longer served her in her life and that she wished to release. All of the women, even those decked out in power suits, followed my directions intently.

Finally, a few heads looked up, then others. On the floor, I had placed a black "burning pot" that looked like a giant soup kettle. I told them, "The fire in this pot symbolizes the ability to release. Fire can transmute things, changing them from one state to another and, in this case, turn something negative into something positive. I will ask each of you to come up here, set fire to those things that you want to release, and drop them into the burning pot. In doing so, you will not only be letting go, you will be clearing space in your life for new things to manifest—new ideas, new relationships, new feelings."

One by one, each woman came up and made her offering to the fire of release. This may sound like a simplistic act, but in actuality it is a very powerful ritual that has been used for centuries to purge the unwanted from one's life. In this case it provided a sense of closure for each woman to end a particular state of being that no longer served her and instead move on to new things.

To my delight, even the most conservative corporate women in the group were deeply touched by this ritual. Several sobbed as they burned their unwanted fears and feelings, symbolically letting go of bad relationships and unproductive patterns. Afterward, many told me that this was one of the most powerful experiences of their lives. Their comments only confirmed what I suspected: People are hungry for ways to connect to the sacred.

Strengthened and encouraged by my initial success, I began to create rituals for all of my workshops. Word spread quickly. Clients began to call asking for my help in creating rituals for new businesses, weddings, baby showers, graduations, job changes, and other types of transitional celebrations, as well as for the ending of relationships and for healing. Time and again, I was struck by the longing that people seemed to have for meaning in their busy and frenetic lives.

ABOUT THIS BOOK

Today rituals are a natural part of my life. In fact, I've created them to mark the most mundane occurrences—like eating a meal or even brushing my teeth. While this may seem a little extreme, the intention is important: *to develop and maintain a habit of mindfulness.* My lectures, tapes, and workshops have inspired thousands of others to do the same.

My intention here is to share my "recipes" with you—to teach you how and when to use ritual as a practical, simple tool to help you cope with problems, gain insights, heighten your intuition, and discover elements of the sacred. I believe that these recipes will enrich and enliven your everyday life while quite literally feeding your soul.

The format of this book resembles a cookbook. Chapter One offers an overview of process and practice. I explain what rituals are and how they create possibilities for bringing you into a sacred space. Chapter Two takes you on a tour of the kitchen. I provide some general guidelines for working with different types of ingredients and for cooking up a ritual. Subsequent chapters will highlight different rituals for special occasions, feelings, or needs. With each, you'll find the ingredients, the recipe, and, when applicable, the follow-up steps. A real-life example—a "ritual reality"—illustrates each recipe.

While I write about the most common uses of ritual, I can't predict the specific events or concerns that may arise in your life. Use my ideas as inspiration, and then use your imagination to create rituals that fulfill your personal needs. Remember that anything can become a ritual, as long as your intention is clear and you set aside the sacred time and space. Then the light of the universe will shine into your heart.

Chapter One
WHAT IS RITUAL?

THE WORD *RITUAL*, DERIVED from an Indo-European root meaning "to fit together," conveys an act in which we literally join the metaphysical with the physical as a means of calling Spirit into our material lives. Rituals also remind us that we have the power to design our lives. Angeles Arrien, author of *The Four-Fold Way,* says, "Ritual is recognizing a life change, and doing something to honor and support the change." Therefore, a ritual of mourning can help us cope with our grief so that we can move forward after the death of a loved one, or a healing ritual can give us additional support to deal with life's challenges. Arrien adds, "In this way, human beings support the changes they are experiencing and create a way to 'fit things together' again." By using rituals, we actively participate in our own development, which enables us to make better sense of things and how they relate to life in general.

If we take the time to stop and bless what we have—our food, our home, our family—we can learn to appreciate each moment and gain happiness from living in the fullness of the present.

Thomas Moore, in *The Education of the Heart,* writes that rituals are "any actions that speak to the soul and to the deep imagination, whether or not it all has practical effects. . . . Even the smallest rites of everyday existence are important to the soul." For example, in South America it is common practice for a mother or grandmother to bless each person as they leave the house in the morning, with the intention of strengthening the family bond as well as each family member's connection to Spirit.

Engaging in a ritual allows your mind to expand, your mood to change, and your spirits to rise. You create smaller symbolic events to represent larger events. Hence, rituals include any kind of *rite* (for example, a christening), *ceremony* (a wedding), *tradition* (hanging stockings), *service* (any action performed in worship, such as the Hindu *puja*, which includes offering flowers to the guru), *liturgy* (the Catholic Mass), *spiritual object* (a Tibetan prayer flag), *mantra* (a sound, like "Om," uttered repeatedly), and even *etiquette* (a handshake, saying "hello" or "thank you"). A ritual is similar to *prayer* as well, in the sense that it encourages us to enter into a state of grace. (In fact, one of the deepest instincts of human beings is to find sprituality.)

Rituals can be used for many purposes—connecting with others, healing, enhancing creativity, ushering in a new life stage, and even simply acknowledging daily routines. They can take seconds or hours. They can be simple or complex, traditional or created in the moment to meet a specific need. They can be performed alone, with one or two other people, or with a large group.

For example, there's an age-old tradition on Broadway called the Gypsy Robe. Before the curtain rises on opening night, the actors join in a circle on the stage. The performer who received the robe at the last Broadway opening is called the Gypsy. He or she steps into the circle and identifies as the new Gypsy the actor with the most theater experience to date. This person dons the robe that has passed from opening to opening, in theater after theater, for the last forty-five years. The new Gypsy walks around the circle three times so that everyone can touch, honor, and bless the robe.

The Gypsy Robe ritual intensifies the connection actors feel with their profession, and at the same time sets the intention for a successful run on Broadway. A veteran actor described this ritual in *The New York Times*, as it occurred before the 1997 revival of *A Funny Thing Happened on the Way to the Forum*: "There is an almost religious feeling on the stage as the many hands reach out to bring luck to the new show. The wearer, as part of the ritual, also visits every dressing room."

In every ritual, we connect to something larger than ourselves, evoking a higher force to be with us. Thus, we are able to bring a sacred feeling to ordinary events, transforming them into times of quiet reflection and connection. They guide us in our day-to-day lives, and lead us to a higher spiritual ground. They mark significant times, ease us through transitions, and—especially in times of rapid change—bring structure and stability into our lives. It's possible to gain valuable, newfound benefits from the ordinary things we already do as well as to heal old wounds, even when the person we hurt or were hurt by cannot participate. Breakfast can become a time when we quiet the mind before a busy day, writing in a journal can release our pent-up emotions, and divorce rituals can give us closure—whether done alone or with an ex-partner.

Most of us regularly participate in rituals. However, we often do them without any thought to their deeper meaning or to their sacred connection to the past. I call these *unconscious* rituals— things we do every day, or at least frequently, like taking a walk, bowling every Thursday night, or eating a Sunday morning pancake breakfast with the children. Sadly, while we do these things often and may even look forward to them as part of our routine, we don't recognize their significance. Even religious rituals can be what I call *rote* rituals. We may participate by attending services and ceremonies rooted in family heritage, but we do so because that's the way things have always been done and not because they mean something to us on a personal level.

Many of the rituals of my childhood, and probably yours, were rote rituals. I grew up in the fifties as a good little Jewish girl living on Long Island. My mother was originally from a Hasidic family. While there was no question that our nuclear family—my parents, brother, sister, and I—was Jewish, we weren't what anyone would call religious. We attended synagogue on the high holy days, fasted on Yom Kippur, and attended Passover seders year after year. I went to Hebrew school where I learned the bits of Jewish history that various holidays commemorated. But I never really felt connected to those rituals. In my preteen years, I went to dozens of friends' Bar Mitzvahs. Beforehand, we teased the boy about his suddenly becoming a man, but we all thought more about what kind of party he'd have or what presents he'd receive than the fact that we

were celebrating an ancient tradition connecting us to our ancestors.

I never questioned these rote rituals; I did them because I was expected to do them. Looking back, however, I realize that although I enjoyed many of the religious traditions of my childhood, the spirit at the heart of each ritual seemed to be missing—much like hearing a beautiful piece of music played slightly off-key. Even as a child, although I couldn't articulate the problem, something felt wrong to me. I sensed that there must be a deeper meaning to those rituals, and I longed to discover it.

WHY WE NEED RITUALS NOW

The truth is, most of us don't give a minute's thought to the *meaning* of the rituals we perform; some people don't honor the rituals of their heritage or religion at all. This, combined with the complexity of today's living, often leads to a sense of emotional or spiritual paralysis. We feel lost and alienated. Our material things—the "toys"—don't yield the kind of happiness we anticipated. We long to return to the time when a wedding truly celebrated a rite of passage, when the birth of a child was blessed as a sacred event, and the lighting of candles signified a real desire to bring light—virtue, healing, and the presence of God—into our homes. We hunger for both community and communion, the feelings found in the *meaningful* practice of rituals. They not only help us make sense of the world and where we fit into it, they also expand our consciousness and connect us to the great mystery of life.

Indeed, the practice of ritual dates back thousands of years. Shinto, the ancient religion of Japan, assumes that everything is alive and that everyone in the world must stay in harmony with nature. In similar ways, forebears from other cultures paid very close attention to their relationship with gods and goddesses and the occurrence of favorable events. They created elaborate rituals to maintain this delicate balance—to ward off the threat of a failed harvest, an earthquake or flood, or any other hardship that could devastate the community.

Transition rituals have been performed throughout time by virtually every civilization. They sanctify everything from the change of seasons to important life passages such as birth, puberty, marriage, and death. It is important for us to recognize, as our ancestors did, that these transitions matter and that rituals support our journey from one state of being to the next. We may act them out in different ways—for example, black signifies bereavement in our society,

while in many Eastern cultures mourners wear white—but their underlying meaning is the same.

Rituals endure because they work. For example, the Zulu culture believes that traditional rituals constitute the family treasure. Neither money nor possessions provide a sense of security—only the rituals passed on to them by their ancestors offer feelings of stability. Among the Amish and the Mormons, Sunday dinners provide important bonding times for children, parents, grandparents, aunts, and uncles by sustaining and strengthening ties to the past. In a landmark study of alcoholic families, Washington, D.C., psychiatrist Steven J. Wolin, M.D., found that despite one or both parents' dysfunction, the continuation of family rituals served as a major protective factor for children. Unfortunately in modern times, particularly in highly industrialized nations like our own, the pendulum has swung from tradition to materialism. Our constant focus on money and material success has led us away from the spiritual and the sacred.

The communication of rituals from one generation to the next resembles a game of Telephone. By the time we do an ancient ritual, its message has been distorted or lost. For example, do you know the original meaning of a bride's wearing something old, something new, something borrowed, and something blue? The "old" symbolized a connection to her ancestors, and the "new" honored the beginning of a relationship. In ancient times, the bride "borrowed" an item from the most fertile woman in her village, thereby assuring the birth of many children. Wearing "blue" signified a connection with the goddess. Did you know that baptism began as a simple rite of purification? Later, it was transformed into a sacrament of initiation, used to bring new members into a religion.

Now, as we approach the twenty-first century, the pendulum is gradually swinging back. The sacred is tugging at our sleeve, urging us to find balance: We must look toward the future with an eye to the past, live in a material world enhanced by the spiritual, and use our heads without denying our hearts. Ritual can help bridge these gaps in easy, uncomplicated ways.

Signs of this change can be seen throughout the world: In the Philippines, when a fire erupts, not only does a fire truck arrive but also a shaman, to exorcise the fire demons—a case of modern technology supported by ancient custom. At the opening ceremony of the 1998 Winter Olympics in Nagano, Japan, event coordinators added an ancient sumo ritual that purified the grounds against *jaki* (evil spirits) and welcomed participants from around the world. Throughout our country, people are turning to feng shui—the Chinese art of placement—to bless and purify a new space. For all of us, in whatever way we choose to express it, believing that there is Spirit in everything will lead to harmony in our environment as well as greater physical and emotional well-being.

Clinical psychologists Hal Stone and Sidra Stone, founders of "voice dialogue therapy," which teaches clients to commune with various aspects of the self, explain that "the use of ritual in our lives provides us with the opportunity to build a bridge between that which is ordinary and that which is extraordinary. It provides a segue between our everyday existence and the reality of the sacred. . . . The use of ritual in our lives brings meaning and focus to our sense of who we are and why we are here on earth."

THE ELEMENTS OF A RITUAL

All rituals—everyday or special-event rituals—have five key elements that work together to create a basic ritual recipe.

Intention

This is the *purpose* of a ritual. You have your morning coffee with the intention of using this time for reflection and relaxation. Or you plan a meaningful anniversary ritual—as opposed to throwing an elaborate party—with the intention of reviewing your years together and renewing your love for each other. What is important is that your intention is pure and that you're sincere.

Sequence

Every ritual has a clear beginning and end. Start with an act, like meditation or lighting a candle, to herald the beginning. At the end, have some form of closure. Most commonly, a moment of quiet reflection acknowledges the experience.

Sacred Space

Because rituals evoke a change of consciousness, they need to take place outside of ordinary life. This isn't difficult to achieve. First of all, *intention* and a clear *beginning* contribute to creating a sacred space. So by simply inhaling a few deep breaths or getting into a tub of warm water, you can transform your everyday environment into ritual space. Of course, you can also go to greater lengths—for instance, by building an altar or making a fire.

Ingredients

Many rituals employ candles, colors, scents, food, music, crystals, objects, and even physical acts as symbolic elements. I have devoted all of Chapter Two to the wide variety of ingredients available.

Personal Meaning

Although this book is chock-full of suggestions, what works for one person may not work for another. Certainly, rituals done for a thousand years have a power of their own and it's important to follow specific steps in re-creating them. But if a ritual has no meaning for you, that power will be lost. It has to signify something in *your* heart to reach *you*. When daily habits become important to us, they take on an almost sacred meaning. Therefore, creating your own personal rituals can have the most power.

You'll be surprised by how easily you can turn an everyday occasion into a ritual. For example, you might already take your daily walk at the same time every day. Your dog comes along, and you always wear the same pair of sneakers. But you don't really *think* about the purpose of your walk—other than seeing it as a good way to give Lassie some exercise. Suppose instead that you intend to make your daily walk a time of self-reflection, so that each step will help put you in tune with your mind and body. Suppose that you now think about the sequence—paying close attention to when the practice begins with tying your sneakers, perhaps rolling your shoulders to loosen up a bit. After your walk, consciously take a few replenishing breaths, drink a glass of water to cleanse your system, and give Lassie a biscuit in appreciation for her accompanying you through the ritual. You'll see that your everyday walk has become a ritual of reflection and rejuvenation.

The same holds true of special-occasion rituals, such as weddings, baby showers, or child-naming ceremonies. Instead of just creating the guest list and planning the menu, slow down and realize that you're participating in a time-honored tradition that connects you to your past. Concentrate on your intention—to commemorate an important rite of passage—and you will get, and give, a deeper meaning and a greater sense of connectedness from each occasion.

WHY RITUALS WORK

Rituals have great power and influence over our minds. As Dr. W. Brugh Joy explains, "There's a part of your psyche that doesn't know the difference between a ritual [and] an actual event." Hence, if you take a ritual bath with the intention of purification, there is a part of you that thinks you have indeed purified yourself, and can now begin anew. Or if you meditate in the morning with the intention of renewal, you will feel more energetic, insightful, and clear because you've told your brain to expect these changes. You can do a ritual to release your anger toward a friend without having to actually talk to the person, or even do a ritual to stop smoking and have your psyche understand it as if you had already stopped.

Think of your brain as a computer into which you constantly download data of equal significance. Your brain cannot distinguish the intensity of meanings. Therefore, when you participate in a ritual, in essence you tell your brain that you already have completed whatever you have enacted symbolically. Visualization techniques work for the same reason. In short, rituals are consciously structured acts intended to influence our subconscious mind. In this way they strengthen our resolve to work toward achieving what we desire.

I recently conducted a ritual workshop during the International Women's Writing Guild Conference at Skidmore College. When I asked the participants to share their writing rituals, they all stared at me blankly. But when I asked what they did to stimulate their creativity, one woman admitted that she donned her special writing shirt. Another had a morning cup of coffee and a walk routine before she sat down at her computer. I suggested that if they added *intention* to the rituals they were already doing, it would spur their writing process.

To help the women make a pledge to honor their writing, I conducted a ritual of commitment, leading them on a guided meditation and then a dialogue with their inner writer. I asked them to write down their intention—what they wanted to receive from this ritual. When the ritual ended, I gave each woman a bracelet and had her take an oath in front of the group as she put it on, promising to make her writing a priority. The women, many in tears, were shocked by the power of the ritual and the information it yielded. Not surprisingly, many of them were told by their inner writer that they had not fully committed themselves to their writing—partners and kids always came first.

Gloria, an eighty-year-old who attended the workshop, was deeply affected by the ritual. She told me that her intention was to find an agent for her new book, but I could see that she still felt skeptical. The next morning, however, she found me at breakfast with a look of sheer joy on her face. Imagine her surprise when another conference participant, who happened to be an agent, approached her and asked if she had any new projects!

While I can't always promise such instant results, rituals do change the dynamics of a situation. For example, although I still feel sadness over my sister's death, I no longer carry the weight of unresolved grief and tension because of the mourning ritual that I've done regularly over the years. Whether you're stuck on a project, burdened by sadness, or paralyzed by fear, an appropriate ritual that has meaning for you will help shift your consciousness.

Rituals aren't magic. However, whether they're done in the privacy of your bedroom or your backyard, the sanctity of a church or temple, or a hall packed with a thousand people, rituals can certainly *seem* magical. They can ease a transition, inspire a new approach to an old problem, help heal the wounds of a bad relationship, and bond a group together.

There's another reason rituals work: *They slow us down.* The Buddhists have a concept called *mindfulness* that embodies this idea, which is about paying attention to the here and now. As we slow down, we gain a new perspective on our lives and are better able to deal with the ups and downs. So many of us spend so much time reliving the past or worrying about the future that we wind up ruining the present. Rituals keep us centered in the present, and at the same time allow us to deal with the past and envision our futures in a very healthy, directed way.

Chapter Two

TOOLS OF THE TRADE

Finding Your Way Around the Kitchen

Aʟʟ ɢᴏᴏᴅ ᴄᴏᴏᴋs ɴᴇᴇᴅ ᴛᴏ learn their way around the kitchen—how to use various utensils and appliances, as well as understand the specific properties of ingredients and what their effect will be when added to a recipe. And certainly, a true chef must have a general idea of the entire process: how to get started, what to do if a particular ingredient is not available, and when the dish is finished. The same process applies to rituals. Before you serve up some of these wonderful delicacies, you'll need to learn about a ritual kitchen.

WHAT'S IN YOUR PANTRY?

Believe it or not, you already have many of the necessary ingredients for creating rituals in your closets, cabinets, and in the natural environment. You'll even find some surprising raw materials in yourself. Let me explain: The ingredients of rituals—symbolic objects, colors, aromas, textures, movements, and sounds—all carry meaning. Some, used for centuries by cultures around the world, have evolved into *universal symbols* with a power of their own. For example, a circle is recognized virtually everywhere to mean wholeness; an egg represents life and rebirth. Other ingredients that you choose for your rituals—a framed photo of your grandmother or a scent that reminds you of a happy time—have *personal* meaning. People often develop rituals based on accessible materials, immediate climate, and living conditions; Hawaiians tend to use the lush flora and ocean surrounding them, while city dwellers gravitate toward indoor rituals.

I will introduce you to the basic provisions in my ritual pantry, and later in this chapter we'll talk about specific ways to use them. I've described the meaning of each ingredient by its most common *Western* interpretation. In our culture, red symbolizes passion, energy, and creation; not many American brides would wear red to their wedding as Chinese brides do!

Remember that these are only guidelines

to get you started. Some of the ingredients may be hard to find if you live in a small town, so I've included (on page 167) a list of mail-order companies from which you can purchase oils, incense, and special music. However, feel free to improvise at any time by using substitutes that you find locally. As you gain confidence, you'll become more creative—just like any good cook.

Candles

For centuries, candles have been lit to welcome Spirit and to symbolize a connection to inner light. The act of lighting a candle creates a sense of serenity and holiness that you may carry into the world. To enhance a candle's power, you can choose a particular color and/or scent.

Colors

Color evokes feeling. As Russian abstract painter Wassily Kandinsky said, "Colors directly influence the soul." Throughout this book, I suggest appropriate colors to incorporate into your rituals through a particular candle, piece of fabric, colored paper, fruit, flower, leaf, or anything else you choose. However, you may have your own interpretation of colors—maybe green reminds you of your mother, who loved wearing it. Honor these associations by adapting them for your own rituals.

COLORS

BLACK: release, the unknown

BLUE: clarity, communication, peace, trust, creativity, innovation

BROWN: earth, grounding, the ability to produce

GOLD: prosperity, strength, courage, self-confidence, the solar principal, the masculine

GREEN: healing, balance, prosperity, harmony, generosity

INDIGO: intuition, trust, feelings, clarity, vision, fearlessness

MAROON: sensuality

ORANGE: joy, sexuality, vitality, spontaneity, optimism, playfulness

PINK: love, compassion

PURPLE: spirituality, inspiration, leadership

RED: passion, energy, creation, stamina,

SILVER: wisdom, fertility, nourishment, growth, the lunar principal, the feminine

TURQUOISE: clarity, peace

YELLOW: power, manifestation, willpower, the intellect, logical thinking

WHITE: purity, universal color for "everything"

Scents

For centuries, people have used plants and their scents in rituals. Today, we call this *aromatherapy*. We draw on the energies of plants and essential oils to create change in our lives. Scientific research confirms their value, proving that scents alone have the power to alter one's state of mind. Aromatherapy consultant John Steele notes, "The *li* [physical manifestation of the life force] of fragrance reveals the hidden depth of things beneath their visible surfaces. At the same time, it elicits insights from our deepest selves that we might never have known."

Aroma has incredible power because, of all five senses, only smell travels directly to the brain. Vanilla might transport you to the safety of your mother's kitchen when you were only three; the scent of chalk can instantly conjure images of your second-grade classroom where you met your favorite teacher; inhaling ocean air may bring back memories of a wondrous vacation with your spouse.

Herbs, spices, and flowers can be found in the form of incense, essential oils, or in their natural state. Look in your local health food store or supermarket, or grow them in your garden. Experiment with different aromas and choose those that mean the most to you—when it comes to incense and essential oils, always try to delight your senses. A healing ritual with lavender oil will not help if lavender brings back negative memories of a despised aunt who terrorized you as a child.

There are many ways to use oils, herbs, flowers, and spices. A release ritual might call for burning herbs such as copal or sage. For certain rituals (such as blessing your office) it might make more sense to combine the herb or oil with water and put it in a spray bottle.

You can release the aroma of essential oils, flowers, herbs, and spices in the following ways:

- Place the oil on a piece of cotton and inhale.

- Pour a few drops of oil in a diffuser, which, like an air freshener, will spread the aroma throughout your home. You can buy three different types of diffusers. One is a small bowl in which you mix the herbs or a few drops of oil with some water, and a candle beneath the bowl heats the contents. The other two kinds are electric. One has a small fan that releases a mist of scented air. The other has a piece of cardboard that is soaked in the scent like a plug-in air freshener. (Diffusers are available in candle shops, New Age stores, or by mail order; see "Sources," page 167.)

SCENTS

BASIL: clarity, success, prosperity

BERGAMOT: peace, relaxation, sleep, opening heart

BLACK PEPPER: protection, energy, courage

CHAMOMILE: peace, relaxation

CINNAMON: prosperity

CITRUS OILS (lemon, grapefruit, orange, lime): joy, purification, revitalization

CLOVES: memory, clarity

COPAL (my personal favorite, usually found in resin form): purification

CYPRESS: comfort (especially for the loss of a loved one), transition

DAFFODIL: new beginnings, transitions

DILL: mental clarity, sharpening the senses

EUCALYPTUS: healing, purification, flexibility

FRANKINCENSE: spirituality, meditation, releasing fear and anxiety

FREESIA: love, peace

GINGER: courage, confidence, male sexual desire

HONEYSUCKLE: prosperity, weight loss

IRIS: love

JASMINE: sexuality, love, facilitating childbirth, clearing obstacles, antidepressant

JUNIPER: health, vitality, purification, inner strength

LAVENDER: calming (good for insomnia), cleansing of karmic patterns and emotional conflicts, helping access grief

LOTUS BLOSSOMS: unrealized dreams

MAGNOLIA: love

MELISSA: soothing, acceptance, strengthening nerves

MIMOSA: dreams

MINT: clarity

NEROLI: joy, uplifting, calm

NUTMEG: prosperity, good luck

PARSLEY: protection

PATCHOULI: aphrodisiac, reduction of frigidity and impotence

PEPPER: courage, energy

PINE, CEDAR, VETEVERT, SPIKENARD: connection to the earth, grounding

ROSE: love, compassion, opening of the heart, enhancing beauty

ROSEMARY: positive change, sharpening memory

SAGE: purification, speaking intentions

SANDALWOOD: relieving anxiety, centering

TULIP: purification

VANILLA: joy, uplifting, relieving of depression

YLANG-YLANG: happiness, sexual energy

- Pour a few drops of oil in a spray bottle filled with water, and spray the fragrant mist around your home.

- Burn a piece of charcoal (which can be purchased in packages of six to eight small, round pieces) in a bowl filled with sand or dirt. Light one side and allow the charcoal to burn through. Then place a few drops of oil or herbs on the smoldering charcoal.

- Herbs, like basil or sage, can be chopped; spices, like peppercorns or cloves, can be crushed. Place them—with or without oil—in a bowl of warm water. Inhale directly or allow the aroma to infuse the room like potpourri.

- Certain herbs, such as sage, cedar, sweetgrass, and lavender, can be "smudged"— bundled up, tied together, lit at one end, and blown out. The smoldering herbs then permeate the air.

- Place a few drops of oil in your bath.

I recommend using only natural oils whenever possible, because synthetic oils don't carry the same vibration. Scott Cunningham explains in his book *Magical Aromatherapy* that "Essential oils are concentrated plant energies, therefore essential oils are powerful reservoirs of natural energies."

Some people have allergic reactions to an herb or fragrance. If you have allergies (or if you are pregnant), don't use essential oils without first checking Robert Tisserand's *The Essential Oil Safety Guide,* or Cunningham's *Magical Aromatherapy* (see "Suggested Reading," page 166). Also remember that to retain their freshness, essential oils should be stored away from heat, light, and moisture.

Food and Drink

Not only are certain rituals related to meals, such as saying grace or conducting a Passover seder, but food itself can also be used symbolically. Many cultures offer food on altars, believing that it will give sustenance to the deities. Ancient Egyptians buried their dead with food because they believed that it nurtured the departed spirit. Hindus and Buddhists shared this belief, and Hindus often used fruit as an offering. On Rosh Hashanah, the Jewish New Year, an apple, symbolizing nature, is dipped in honey to bring sweetness into the coming year. Native Americans use corn or cornmeal to signify the abundance of a harvest. Often, when we visit a new home, we bring bread, sugar, and salt, signifying nourishment, sweetness, and purification.

Of course, many edibles also carry personal meanings. We all have our favorite comfort foods (the healing property of chicken soup is almost

∽ FOOD ∽
AND DRINK

BREAD, RICE, CORN, GRAINS: earth, harvest, abundance

CAKE: celebration, sweetness

CITRUS FRUITS: joy, vitality

EGGS: bounty, spiritual renewal, rebirth

FRUIT: abundance, health, potential

HONEY, SUGAR, MOLASSES, CHOCOLATE: sweetness

HOT SPICES: sexuality, creativity

ICE: frozen emotions

MANGOES: sensuality

MILK: nurturing, sustenance

OYSTERS: sensuality, hidden beauty

POMEGRANATE: rebirth

POPCORN: creativity, new ideas

SALT: purification

SEEDS: new potential

WATER: emotions, subconscious, source of life, purification

WINE AND GRAPE JUICE: celebration, bounty, abundance

RED WINE: the power of women's menstrual blood, creation of new life

WHITE WINE: the power of men and the creation of new life

universally recognized). We can use food to represent where we live, where we came from, and its meaning to us and our loved ones. For example, if I were doing a grief ritual for my father who died in 1994, I might incorporate his beloved halvah. I've included a list of some of the most common foods and drinks that you can use in rituals.

M u s i c ∽

An important aspect of rituals, music helps create or alter a mood, touching your physical, emotional, and spiritual being. Anyone who has attended a rock concert or a classical music recital experiences the power of music to transform. Songs with a repeating chorus, chant, or mantra can produce trancelike states. Music unites people as well; when twenty thousand voices sing the national anthem at a ball game, the entire crowd becomes one.

Certain rhythms emulate a heartbeat and their repetition can help us balance. We learn from Angeles Arrien's book *The Four-Fold Way* that research conducted by Andrew Neher shows "the sonic driving of the drum can affect the alignment of the brain, resonating frequency with external auditory stimuli. This alignment can rebalance the central nervous system."

Music enhances ritual. Experiment with different kinds to evoke the mood you wish to create. Choose joyful sounds for celebrations, calming tones for healing rituals, and sacred music for weddings or rites of passage. Try chants and prayers in other languages; you'll be amazed to find that even though you don't understand the words, you'll feel the *feelings*. And of course you should use personal favorites, too—for example, an anniversary ritual will mean more to both partners when "your" song is playing.

Crystals

A crystal is an earth element, a mineral or gemstone. Both ancient cultures and modern science have utilized the mysterious qualities of crystals.

~ CRYSTALS AND GEMSTONES ~

AMETHYST: spiritual awareness, transmutation, healing

AQUAMARINE: purification, healing, calming

BLOODSTONE: courage, physical energy

CALCITE: balance, peaceful meditation

CARNELIAN: sex, self-esteem, creativity

COPPER: purification, inspiring love, making peace

FLUORITE: healing, releasing unwanted energies

GOLD: courage, self-awareness, self-confidence, wealth, virtue

HEMATITE: willpower, concentration

JADE: fertility, wisdom, tranquility

LAPIS LAZULI: communication, healing

MALACHITE: protection, money

MOONSTONE: love, psychic awareness

NICKEL: youth, beauty, growth, adaptation

OBSIDIAN: inner growth, psychic development

OPAL: passion, love, emotional expression

PEARL: purity, integrity, focus, wisdom

QUARTZ: change, focus

ROSE QUARTZ: love, compassion

SILVER: fertility, nourishment, growth

TIGER'S-EYE: empowerment, willpower, courage, clarity

TIN: flexibility

TOPAZ: new beginnings

TOURMALINE: healing, balance

TURQUOISE: balance, connection with all life, friendship, positive thinking

Egyptians, Australian aboriginals, and Native Americans used them in healing rituals, and they now serve as the cornerstone of digital technology in our own information age.

Crystals have the ability to receive and transmit energy. They are powerful focusing tools. They can assist you in rituals of healing, manifesting your vision, and transmuting negative emotions. But remember, they are only *tools* that can aid you in attaining a deeper level of understanding. Crystals have the power to help you, but don't give away your own power and expect them to do all the work.

Objects and Artifacts

Carl Jung theorized that symbols go directly into the brain, connecting you with the past. In almost every ritual, you will use objects that carry certain meaning. Some will evoke what Joseph Campbell calls your "personal mythology," stories that have been handed down from generations past, the sum of which adds up to where you came from and who you are. You can use traditional religious symbols, such as a statue of the Blessed Mother, pictures of angels, a Buddhist prayer wheel, or artifacts from other cultures like a Native American talking stick. The objects you use in a ritual are limited only by your imagination.

Don't forget about the everyday materials that you keep around the house. The following are some useful items that you can use in creating your rituals.

EVERYDAY MATERIALS

ART SUPPLIES
(crayons, colored markers, paint, clay)

BEADS

CARDBOARD SHOE BOXES

FEATHERS

FABRIC AND RIBBON

PERSONAL TREASURES
(such as photos and jewelry)

SEWING NEEDLES AND THREAD

SCISSORS

SHELLS, ROCKS, LEAVES, TWIGS

SILK FLOWERS, PIPE CLEANERS

STRING, YARN

TAPE AND GLUE

Physical Acts

Certain activities are performed in ritual to quiet the mind and imprint new behavioral patterns. Jews rock back and forth when they *daven* (pray); Sufis whirl; Hindus and Buddhists assume certain yoga positions that affect the mind and body—for example, the sun salutation, and *mudras*, which are sacred hand movements. These acts enhance your journey into a heightened state of awareness. For Hawaiian dancers, each hand gesture in the hula is sacred; in Bali, even the shifting of eyes is intrinsic to a dance ritual. You don't need special training to experience magic in physical acts. Singing, chanting, humming, dancing, and reciting poetry, as well as repetitive movements like pounding, drumming, rocking, swaying, or shaking a rattle can be incorporated into the rituals you design. These acts help to break up rigidity and old forms, allowing you to be more open and focused on the ritual.

THE ELEMENTS OF NATURE

Traditional rituals are connected to the cycles in nature. They always include the four elements: fire, water, air, and earth. For example, when a shaman from almost any indigenous culture performs a ritual, he literally calls in the spirits of the East, West, North, and South, each of which corresponds to one of the four elements. In the moving meditations of tai chi and qi gong, each posture evokes these elements. Different cultures attribute different qualities to the directions. In some systems East represents fire, while in others South

represents fire. The attributions I use are those recognized in northern Europe.

Many ancient and modern rituals are conducted in circles that represent life's continuity; participants position themselves according to the direction they wish to invoke. For example, a marriage ceremony takes place in the southern area of the circle, the place of passion and heart energy, while a puberty ritual occurs in the east, representing new beginnings.

When we design rituals, the same primary objective holds: to join with these natural elements of the universe, the source of all life. Energy is there for us, if we know how to tap into it. Each of the four elements represents an ability, a mind-set, and a strength. It is also associated with a particular direction, time of day, season, scent, color, animal, and object.

Air

Communication, the mind, learning, psychic work, travel, overcoming addictions

DIRECTION: east
TIME OF DAY: dawn
SEASON: spring
SCENTS: basil, bergamot, mint, dill, parsley
COLORS: yellow, white
ANIMAL: eagle

OBJECTS: feathers, wind chimes

MINERALS: amber, topaz, citrine

Fire ⌒

Transformation, purification, growth, sexuality, passion, will

DIRECTION: south

TIME OF DAY: noon

SEASON: summer

SCENTS: frankincense, copal, black pepper, clove, lime, rosemary, ginger

COLORS: red, orange

ANIMALS: coyote, mouse

OBJECTS: candles, bonfires, hot peppers

MINERALS: ruby, garnet, carnelian, bloodstone

Water ⌒

Fluidity, purification, renewal, deep unconscious, emotions, compassion, primeval womb, the deep feminine, fertility

DIRECTION: west

TIME OF DAY: dusk

SEASON: autumn

SCENTS: sandalwood, chamomile, freesia, iris, jasmine, rose, vanilla, ylang-ylang

COLORS: blue, green, turquoise, indigo

ANIMALS: bear, raven

OBJECTS: glass, cup, bowl, ocean, river, lake, stream, juice, wine

MINERALS: pearl, moonstone, obsidian, amethyst, opal

Earth ⌒

Nurturing, the body, material possessions, natural cycles, structure

DIRECTION: north

SEASON: winter

TIME OF DAY: midnight

COLORS: brown, green

SCENTS: pine, cedar, vetevert, spikenard, honeysuckle, lilac

ANIMALS: buffalo, white owl

OBJECTS: plants, flowers, dirt, salt, grains, bread

MINERALS: emerald, turquoise, malachite, chrysocolla

THE RAW MATERIALS: YOUR MIND AND BODY

Within each of us lies an untapped source of peace, wisdom, and guidance. We often don't realize this, however, until we slow down, quiet our minds, tune in to our bodies, and allow the creative juices to flow. The following basic techniques, to which I refer throughout this book, can help you do just that.

Conscious Breathing ~

This is an important part of almost every ritual because it calms you and helps bring you into a sacred space. Many types of breathing exercises are practiced in various schools of meditation; particular kinds of breathing will refresh or relax you, make you more alert, or put you to sleep.

Use whichever breathing practice feels most comfortable. For those of you who've never meditated or tried ritual relaxation or visualization, the following is a basic breathing technique.

Sit quietly, making sure that your back is supported by a comfortable cushion, and close your eyes. Take a deep breath through your nose, gently inhaling as much air as possible into your body. Since this is probably the first conscious breath you've taken today, enjoy it. Allow the breath to move deep into your belly, filling it with air, expanding it. Some people call this a "belly breath." Then exhale slowly. Continue breathing in through your nose to the count of four, hold for the count of two, and exhale slowly to the count of four. Take slow deep breaths and focus only on your breathing—in and out, in and out, in and out. Repeat until you feel calm and relaxed. Learning how to breathe is the first step toward meditation.

Meditation ~

I begin each day by spending at least twenty minutes meditating. However, sitting still may not appeal to you. That's okay. You can attain a relaxed, meditative state in many other ways—walking, swimming, gardening, or simply lying on the ground and watching the clouds roll by. It can be done in absolute quiet or with music, in privacy or with a group, indoors or out. To relax the mind, you may also choose to repeat a simple word, like *peace* or *om*, as you breathe.

Relaxation not only calms you, it puts you into a *heart-centered* space. It allows your innate compassion and love to guide you, instead of letting the often critical and overanalytical mind run the show. If you focus on your heart for a minute or two, the chaos in your mind will quiet and you will establish a deeper relationship with your inner wisdom and heighten your capacity to heal. The most profound connections take place within the heart.

Visualization/ Guided Imagery ~

The deepest part of your imagination is an untapped resource. Learn to harness its power. In countless studies, scientists have proven that you can actually have a conversation with your body; in turn, it talks to your brain, which then directs your nervous system's response. *Calm down. Be confident. Be proud of yourself. Heal. Think of new solutions.* The more you send positive messages, the more you will manifest good health and enhanced experience.

Visualization serves as a means to transmit these messages. Successful visualization allows your body to move into the so-called relaxation response—your heart slows, your mind clears, your muscles relax. Some people naturally do this better than others—psychologists refer to them as "high absorbers," people who direct their bodies with their minds more easily.

But remember that mastering visualization is a *process*; you'll get better with practice. I have worked with people who at first could barely conjure the image of white light, and now they see specific pictures in Technicolor. (You may never actually *see* pictures, but chances are you will find other ways to visualize—hearing sounds or feeling sensations.)

What, exactly, *is* visualization? I think of it as a self-told story that calms your body and sets your mind in a particular direction—a way of connecting your mind, body, and spirit. A visualization can relax or heal you, dredge up emotions that you need to release, ease anxiety, inspire creativity, and provide guidance.

You can follow someone else's script or create your own visualization. If you do make up your own, you may want to make an audiotape of it so that you can play it back and peacefully experience its power. Guided imagery can include any or all of the following components:

⬧ **Going to a special space**—You can choose to be in a garden, at the beach, in the woods, at a historical site you've been to or read about, on a space capsule zooming through the heavens, or any imaginary place, as long as it is *yours* and feels safe.

⬧ **Engaging all your senses**—When you've arrived at that special place, what do you see and hear? What scents and textures surround you? A high absorber might even be able to taste the experience. The more you engage all your senses, the faster your body responds and the more effective the exercise will be.

⬧ **Contacting a "Wisdom Figure"**—Picture someone you have known, a family elder, a teacher, a spiritual leader or mythological figure, a religious symbol, or simply colors and light that seem to lead to wisdom. My figure is generally a sage—an ageless woman with very strong features and an imposing frame. She is all-knowing and utterly compassionate. For me, she embodies the wisdom of the ages. Other people don't necessarily see anything, but they sense a presence. One woman even saw Abraham Lincoln! Be open to the endless possibilities. Your wisdom figure may be a surprise, or, he/she/it may change over time.

⬧ **Asking for guidance**—Once you have

connected with your own wisdom figure, ask any questions that come to mind. *What should I do next? Why do I feel this way? Am I on the right track? Is there something I need to know right now? What will make me feel fulfilled?* You may have a specific question for a particular problem. Ask away.

CREATING AN ALTAR

We tend to think of an altar as something found in a house of worship. That's true—but why can't you also have one in your own house? One of the best ways I know to bring the sacred into your everyday life is to create an altar. You can have one in your home, office, school, or car; it will transport you away from everyday concerns and connect you to something larger than yourself.

Creating an altar is integral to most rituals. The symbols you choose to place on your altar will reinforce your intention. For example, in a prosperity ritual, you can feature money. In a healing ritual (see page 126), a photo of the patient—happy and well—can be powerful. Even if you do none of the rituals in this book, an altar will constantly remind you that a divine presence works in your life. That is why nomadic people keep portable altars.

Your altar should reflect you and your dreams, so make it uniquely yours. Think of it as a message board to the universe—a way of sending direct communications to God. An old friend, Carol, wrote *joy, fun, dance,* and *dream* on rocks and placed them on her altar. Evelyn has pictures of her spiritual teachers and close friends, and she regularly lights incense and candles. My son, Jourdan, has a collection of crystals, along with a picture of his pet cats. Rena, a writer, includes her screenplays and novels as part of her offerings. On my own altar, I have fresh flowers, a candle, a statue of Kuan Yin (the Chinese goddess of compassion), a shell that represents the earth and reminds me of a beach that I love, pictures of my family, and positive affirmations I've written down. In honor of the elements, I light incense (symbolizing both fire and air) and I always keep a small dish of water to symbolize fluidity.

You can also have a group or family altar, with each person placing something that is special to them on it, thus weaving individuals together to provide a sense of wholeness and connection.

Altars can be permanent, temporary, and/or portable: A *permanent altar* can be established on a chest, a small table, or the floor. Find a spot that won't be disturbed—a table or a corner of your desk. Place a cloth over the area, then fill your altar with meaningful symbols: pictures of your loved ones, an object that connects you to nature (like a shell, a leaf, or a stone), a reminder of a teacher or wise, loving friend. If you want to strengthen your connection to Spirit, include a religious figure or symbol, and try to have something signifying each element—fire, water, air, earth.

Your attention will be energized by the objects you choose to place on the altar, so select items that matter to you—make it personal and beautiful. Each time you glance at the altar, it will remind you of the things that are most important to you and of the support available to you. You can change it weekly, seasonally, or whenever you feel the need to bring in new energy or ideas. Sacred space that is used repeatedly over time builds emotional, energized charges. (Anyone who has ever visited Notre Dame Cathedral in Paris, the Wailing Wall in Jerusalem, or other revered monuments can confirm this.)

A *temporary altar* is one that you create for a specific ritual. Set it up wherever you think it will have the greatest power—for example, in your bedroom for a sensuality ritual (see page 133). Don't be afraid to be adventurous. Some of my favorite items come from toy stores and craft fairs. Use natural settings—arrange stones around a tree or seashells and seaweed at the shore.

A *portable altar* should fit into a small box or case that is easy to carry. It can include a candle, a symbol of Spirit, some incense, a vial of essential oils, or a beautiful cloth.

Some rituals don't require an altar in the strictest sense of the word and are more spontaneous and flexible. However, it is always a good idea to use an altar when you can to increase the ritual's power.

Remember to keep your altar as a place of reverence. Don't leave coffee mugs or yesterday's mail on it. Let it be an environment in which everyday moments can become precious jewels, manifesting as pure, invisible Spirit.

GETTING STARTED

Once you've become familiar with the implements, ingredients, and raw materials in your pantry, you're ready to cook. The next three steps are preparation (put on that apron), process (get down to business), and follow-up (enjoy the finished product).

The first step involves *intention*. As I discussed in the Introduction, intention is one of the key elements of a ritual. Why do you want to do this ritual? What do you hope to gain from it? Remember that rituals should be done with an open heart—*never* to manipulate another human being. Take a few moments and write down the answers. Be clear and careful. For example, if you plan a release ritual (see page 98), ask yourself if you *really* want to release the person, relationship, job, or habit; try to imagine how it will change your life.

If you are doing a ritual with others, talk with them about content. It's hard for anyone to focus on a ritual if he or she doesn't understand what's going on. Explain exactly what you are going to do ahead of time, so that everyone involved can participate at the deepest level.

Next, *assemble your ingredients.* I've given you an entire supermarket full of ingredients that you might include, but don't get caught up in having it be perfect. If you can't find an object, draw a picture of it, sculpt it out of clay, carve it out of wood, or simply cut a picture out of a magazine. If the recipe calls for a yellow candle and you can't find one, use white, the universal color. Think of creating rituals as making soup. I can give you the basics, but it is up to you to season it to your own taste. And remember, never do anything that contradicts your own belief system.

Where will you conduct your ritual? Location can affect the quality of your experience. Whether it's a backyard, living room, bedroom, or office, the area should be free from distractions and interruptions. Turn off the phone and fax machine. Hang a "DO NOT DISTURB" sign on your door.

Remember that a ritual must have a *sacred space* (page 15). The simple act of lighting a candle, burning incense, ringing a bell, or sprinkling salt or water can sanctify a space. Some people remove their shoes when entering a ritual space or wash their hands with scented water to symbolize leaving the outside world for a brief moment in time. I always have a bowl of sage water near my front door for my friends to wash their hands. This eases the transition from the outside noise of New York City to a quiet and calm atmosphere.

You also need to have a clear sense of *beginning and ending* (see page 15). You can turn on music, light a candle, take a deep breath, or just say "I am now beginning." Close your eyes and find your heart center as you embark on your journey. Your ritual must have a formal ending, too: Blow out the candle, say "thank you" or "amen," or have a quiet moment of reflection, followed by a deep breath.

In many rituals, I include a *follow-up* suggestion. Remember, rituals are symbolic rites that unlock doors to a new awareness, healing, and state of being. But a ritual is only the key that opens the door. Once you walk through, you must find ways to continue the process and create new patterns for success. Smoking cessation research shows that it takes twenty-one days to change a habit. Most new behaviors need at least that long to take hold.

You might repeat rituals or take other steps to reinforce your change. Ask others to respect the transition and to help you continue on your new path. In particular, when you leave behind a negative habit, it's vitally important to create new patterns of behavior to replace the old. Support groups can offer added stability.

Follow-up suggestions vary. For example, in one of the rituals designed to help you get in touch with your sensual self, I suggest that you wear something sensual the next day—silky underwear, special perfume, or a flowing chiffon scarf. If you have a community ritual (see page 112) with the intent of connecting people, plan another event within the next few months. And some rituals, such as those celebrating an event, do not always require any follow-up.

POINTS TO REMEMBER

Here are a few final bits of advice before you set off on your ritual journey:

Keep it simple

When you begin to create rituals, make them simple and clear. You can get more intricate as you gain confidence. Don't let material constraints—not having exactly the right object or the perfect space—detract from creating meaningful experiences. Let that principle be a metaphor for your life: Never base your well-being on factors outside of you or out of your control.

Include the children

Children love to help out in the kitchen—the *ritual* kitchen as well. I encourage you to share these rites and ceremonies with them. Ask your own children to contribute their ideas. Kids have a natural inclination toward ritual; their imagination lends creativity and inspiration that will delight and amaze you. Do not assume that kids are too young to appreciate rituals. On the contrary, rituals will provide a welcome sense of structure and continuity.

Be open to new possibilities

As you participate in rituals, you will notice that the universe lends its support so that miracles can occur. You will gain new insight into your life, healing will take place, and energy blocks will crumble. Think of yourself as tuning in to the universal life force. See your life as a great adventure—follow a new route home, taste a new food, try something you've never done before. Imagine yourself as a tourist visiting a foreign country. Look at your life with fresh eyes and discover its hidden treasures.

Chapter Three
EVERYDAY RITUALS

MOST OF THE TIME WE MOVE through our days on automatic pilot, mindlessly racing from one responsibility to the next, from one person's demands to another's, from one busy area of our lives to an entirely different—but just as busy—area. We often don't stop to consider what we're doing, how we're doing it, or even why. And we certainly don't take time to breathe, let alone to "smell the roses." No wonder we're plagued with backaches, headaches, anxiety, and ulcers. I have found that everyday rituals provide a powerful antidote to this stress. They help me to slow down and be more aware of myself in my environment, bringing a soothing sense of inner calm to everything I do. They can do the same for you.

The tangled complications of work and relationships will begin to unravel as you weave simple, everyday rituals into your routine. You'll discover peace and quiet in which to renew your strength, experience clarity and a sense of self-confidence, or find a private moment to breathe deeply before you confront the next task.

The following rituals are some of my favorites. Many of my clients and friends practice these on a regular basis, with slight variations, to meet their own needs and circumstances. They may not seem like rituals in a formal sense, in that some can be done without particular ingredients, or symbolic elements, or an altar. All you need is your conscious awareness, time, and the intention of connection with yourself or others. I also recommend that, whenever possible, you do remember to take time to connect with your altar of choice—ideally, once a day. After all, it is a focal point for connecting to Spirit.

Morning

HOW MANY NIGHTS DO YOU crawl into bed thinking, "This day started off badly and just kept getting worse"? How do you sleep after inevitably reviewing the mix-ups and mess-ups that filled your day? And how do you greet the next morning? Emotionally hungover? Too depleted to make the new day any different from the one before?

A morning ritual helps you begin each day with peace and optimism, believing in your own ability to cope with whatever awaits you out there in the world. Time for yourself can change the entire energy of your day; it can clarify your perceptions as it enriches your physical, emotional, and intellectual resources.

Intention ⌒
To center yourself in a moment of inner quiet and become familiar with how you feel in a calm, focused state, so that you can recall it as needed—for additional energy and inspiration—during the day.

Timing ⌒
Every morning, before starting your busy day.

Ingredients ⌒
Citrus oil—orange, grapefruit, lemon (optimism and joy), bowl of warm water; you can also use the fruit itself.

Recipe ⌒
Consciously begin each day expecting the best. At first this may be difficult but it will get easier, especially as you wake up anticipating the pleasure of your morning ritual. Set aside a special time (as short as five minutes, or longer if you can) just for yourself. Place a few drops of citrus oil into the bowl of warm water on your altar. With each breath, inhale the uplifting fragrance.

Remember, this ritual is your own. You can choose to be very still, looking at something that gives you pleasure—a photograph of an old friend, a beautiful painting, or the view from your window. You can close your eyes and listen to a favorite piece of music, recite a poem that you love, or say a short prayer for someone in your life, even for yourself. If you choose to be active—walking, arranging flowers, or working on a model airplane—take a few moments at the beginning and end of your ritual to breathe the citrus aroma.

RITUAL REALITY

Recognizing that he requires quiet time to bridge the gap between sleep and the hustle and bustle of his day, John has structured an outdoor ritual to meet his needs. He begins by peeling and eating an orange, tasting and smelling the rich aroma. Then he dresses in the clothes he's set out for himself the night before and quietly leaves his house. Rain or shine, at all times of the year, John walks the few blocks to his neighborhood park. Once there, he purposefully savors all of the seasonal colors, textures, and aromas the park offers. He inhales the frostiness of winter, the lushness of summer, the newness of spring, and the bittersweet crispness of autumn. John consciously connects with the earth. He tells friends that he experiences a specific strength from this ritual, one that affects his spirit, body, and mind throughout the day.

With time, John also noticed the long-term benefits of his morning ritual. By developing a deeply personal relationship with nature's cycles, he now has a greater capacity for change and growth in his own life, as well as a firm confidence in his ability to weather the fluctuations such change might bring. Further, John enjoys a richer appreciation for the arts because of his attention to the beauty of the park.

Appreciation

WHEN SERIOUS ILLNESS strikes a family member or friend, we suddenly realize how much we value them in our lives and we also think about the importance of our own health. We become more sensitive to the goodness in our lives. Simple things take on new meanings—the taste of a crisp apple, the sweetness of a child's smile, the thoughtfulness of a friend. Life seems more precious, and we become more conscious that our time on earth is limited and that we need to value every moment.

Why does it take a tragedy to make us appreciate what we have? Why can't we be aware, on a daily basis, of the opportunities that surround us to love, to learn, and to care about the well-being of others and ourselves? This ritual will help you cope when faced with difficulties—great *and* small. It is designed to weave into your daily life feelings of appreciation and to help you feel grateful, even when you're sad or fearful.

Intention
To value and honor those you love and yourself.

Timing
At least once a week.

Ingredients
Essence of cinnamon or cinnamon sticks (prosperity and abundance), small bowl of water, notebook and pen, stationery.

Recipe
To begin, pour a few drops of essence of cinnamon into a diffuser or spray bottle, or crush two cinnamon sticks into the small bowl of warm water, which can go on your altar. Allow the aroma to permeate your space. Now list your material possessions—your home, car, clothes, books, food, television, computer, and so on. You will probably be surprised by what you actually *have*. Write one or two reasons why each is important to you. Now list memories that have stayed with you—of places you've been, paintings you've seen, music you've heard—and why all of these matter to you.

Finally, make a list of the people in your life, from friends and family to coworkers and others you encounter on a regular basis. Next to each one write two or three things that you appreciate about them, such as your next-door neighbor's cheerful "Hello," the patient service from the clerk in the hardware store, your partner's love, the wisdom of a teacher, or the dependable understanding from your oldest friend.

With some people it may be more of a challenge for you to find qualities to appreciate. Remember, even if someone has a harsh or negative attitude, a valuable lesson may be hiding somewhere. The Chinese have understood this concept for thousands of years; their calligraphers have always written the word "crisis" by joining the symbols for danger and opportunity. When hostility is directed at you, you can see it as a chance to strengthen your boundaries and stand up for yourself and what you believe in. You may not view the event positively when it happens, but the more often you practice this ritual, the more quickly you'll recognize the value of such a moment.

When you first do this ritual, it may take some time. But once you've made your lists, you can continually update them. And the next time you're ready to do this appreciation ritual, everything you need will be right there, ready for your review.

If you don't have much time but want to take a few minutes to reflect on the good in your life, Hawaiians have a wonderful blessing ritual, similar to my appreciation ritual. As they walk around, they bless everything they see: flowers for their fragrant perfume, roads for supporting them, clothes for their beauty and protection, and local dogs for their loyalty. By focusing on something positive, in effect, they change their own vibration; as they bless things, they actually open themselves up to receive more blessings.

RITUAL REALITY

Jack said good-bye to the corporate world to start a career as a freelance writer. He came to me one afternoon feeling scared and not knowing what to do. He was running out of money and beginning to panic. He said, "Nothing seems to be working out. Everything in my life feels just plain *bad*." I suggested that we try the appreciation ritual and told him to write a list of all of his resources.

He laughed and said, "That should take about a minute and a half!" But he began to write, starting with the people in his life. He was surprised by how many people he thought of and how easily he found reasons for valuing them— their advice, understanding, and patience, or invitations to dinner and weekends in the country. For his possessions, Jack wrote down his apartment and its furnishings, and his new laptop that allowed him to work wherever he wanted.

I asked if he had enough money to pay his rent and take care of his needs (not necessarily his wants). Jack said that he did have enough for now, but he was really worried about the future. I encouraged him to focus on the present and to keep the list in his pocket to reassure him whenever he felt alone and adrift. Jack sighed deeply and the worry lines in his face disappeared as he started to see the universe as a place that offered him abundance and freedom. Jack said that he planned to express his deep appreciation to all of those people who had given him so much.

I told him about an ancient metaphysical belief called the "tenfold return," whereby what you give will be replaced tenfold. It follows the notion that the universe fills empty spaces, so you should always make room for new things to come into your life.

Jack left and I didn't hear from him for nearly a week. Then he called to tell me a story. The day after our meeting he gave five dollars to a musician playing his violin in front of a newsstand. Two days later, Jack's friend Janice gave him a twenty-five-dollar ticket to a concert he really wanted to attend. Of course, some giving doesn't manifest its rewards so literally, but this story does illustrate the notion rather well.

F o l l o w - U p

When you finish, review the people you've listed and write or call at least one of them to say how much you appreciate them. You might even send flowers or a tin of homemade cookies just to thank them for being in your life. Another way to express appreciation is through tithing, giving 10 percent of your earnings to your religious institution or to a cause that you believe in. Metaphysically and emotionally, the more you give, the more you will receive.

Inner Guidance

WHEN WE ARE GROUNDED in the present moment—our place, our time, our feelings—we can make authentic choices that are based upon our spiritual needs. We can act appropriately, responding to what we truly need and want, instead of doing what we think we *should* do. Remember, many of our *shoulds* come from another place and time when we ourselves were different. Living in the here and now, we find we have a better response to our lives, and certainly greater enthusiasm and energy. Think about how you feel when you spend time with someone out of obligation, rather than because you want to. We all know the importance of regular physical examinations. But what about regular spiritual and emotional exams? This ritual will help you to look closely at how you feel and what you need. You will have more energy, clarity, and caring to offer others if you give them to yourself first.

Intention
To connect to your true sense of self.

Timing
At best, every day; at least once a week; when you feel out of touch with your own needs.

Ingredients
Mint (clarity, clearing blocks), indigo candle (intuition), small bowl, paper, pen or pencil, markers or crayons.

Recipe
Find a quiet time and place where you won't be disturbed and set up your altar. Light the candle and crush the mint in the bowl. As you begin, and throughout the ritual, inhale the minty fragrance. Now focus on your heart center for thirty seconds (see page 28). Then, write these phrases, leaving plenty of space after each one: *I feel* _____, *I need* _____, *I want* _____.

Allow yourself to fill in the blanks freely, moving about from feelings to needs to wants. Don't censor yourself or worry about spelling or grammar.

Adding colors for emphasis, or to express a mood, may enhance your process—green may bring you comfort, brown may signify a need to ground your energy. Appreciate the freedom of knowing you are the only one who will see these pages.

Your emotions might range from profound sadness to childlike silliness. You may also wish for a longer period than you had planned for this ritual; schedule it when more time is a viable option. Think of this as a "mapping" ritual that will lead you back to yourself and to your own creativity, power of determination, and inner strength.

RITUAL REALITY

Everyone loved Susan. At thirty-eight she was an exemplary wife, mother of three young children, and a loyal friend with a kind word for everyone. A master juggler, she managed to head the hospital volunteers, act as secretary of the PTA, and lead her daughter's Girl Scout troop. However, she woke up almost every morning with a headache.

When Susan came to me, she complained that her energy level felt lower and lower, and that she grew increasingly irritated by the smallest provocations. Susan listened with a mixture of skepticism and curiosity when I explained the Inner Guidance Ritual. The next morning after her husband and children left the house, Susan turned off her telephone, locked her front door, took out a notebook and pencil, and sat down on her back porch. "I saw tulips and daffodils blooming that I didn't even remember planting," she told me later. "It was the first time in months that I'd stopped long enough to take a deep breath, let alone to feel what I really felt!"

As soon as Susan began to write, the truth came tumbling out. "I feel tired. I feel burned out. I feel like I'm going a million miles per hour on a merry-go-round." She paused for a moment and then added, "I feel sad. I feel unfulfilled. . . ." She stood up, took off her shoes, and walked through the cool morning grass, notebook in hand. She wrote, "I need a break. I need time to myself. I need music."

Surprised both by the power of her feelings and the fact that they had come tumbling out so quickly, Susan slowly reread what she had written. She then imagined herself at her happiest— as a girl playing the piano, accompanying her friends as they sang the latest Broadway tunes. Why couldn't she re-create this scene in the present with her husband and children?

"There is no doubt," Susan says now, "that doing this ritual was an important turning point in my life." She laughs, "And my family's! You should hear my husband and kids belting out those songs!"

Journal Writing

WRITING ABOUT OUR FEELINGS and impressions gives us a unique understanding of ourselves. Neither talking with others nor thinking in solitude provides the distinctive comfort and clarity that comes from writing and then reading and rereading our own words on a page.

Writing is also freeing. It allows us to express and get rid of things that weigh us down and slow us up; it is enlightening, because our ideas and emotions often surprise us. With time, you will learn to appreciate your own innate truth and wisdom. You will delight in your own creativity and growing self-knowledge, and in the confidence they bring.

Intention
To gain clarity through self-awareness.

Timing
When you feel the need for understanding.

Ingredients
Essence of sandalwood, lavender, or melissa (calmness), green candle (harmony), journal, pen, your favorite music, and symbolic item that you will use only for this ritual (see below).

Recipe
Establish a familiar space for yourself and take out your special writing item—a beautiful spiral-bound notebook, a "writing cushion" to support your back, or a cozy "writing shawl" to wrap around your shoulders. This notifies your psyche that you are ready to begin the ritual and commit yourself to writing. Make sure that no one will disturb you. Many of my clients have found that when they schedule this practice very early in the morning or late at night before going to sleep they have more privacy.

Create an altar with the candle and essences you have chosen. Light the candle and take three or four slow, deep breaths, appreciating the aroma of your essence. Meditate or use a visualization technique as suggested on pages 28-30. Then, simply begin to write any images, ideas, and feelings that enter your head, in any order they come to you. Don't worry about making sense; it's okay to interrupt or contradict yourself. Some people call this "automatic" or "twilight" writing. At first it may feel awkward. Your words may seem baffling or even incoherent. But trust the process and, most of all, yourself. You will be amazed by the emerging insights that come from the freedom of expressing yourself honestly and without self-consciousness.

RITUAL REALITY

Every morning following my meditation time, I brew a small pot of chamomile tea to enhance my sense of peace and relaxation. While I wait for it to steep, I set out my special cup and saucer, my journal opened to a new page, and my pen. The stillness of the morning, the memory of my meditative insights, and the familiar flavor and aroma of the tea encourage me to connect with myself through writing.

But not everyone approaches journal writing the same way. My old friend Sam is one of those people who easily grasps a broad concept, discards any particulars someone else has attached to it, and then makes it distinctly his own.

Sam's brokerage office is located in the heart of Chicago's loop. Everyday after the stock market closes and before he finishes writing up his daily report, he grabs his briefcase, waves to his secretary with the promise to return in forty-five minutes, and takes the elevator down to one of the noisiest streets in America. He walks a few steps to a dilapidated diner, where he slides into his regular booth. "The usual," he says to the familiar waiter, who quickly brings him his piece of apple pie and cup of hours-old coffee. From his briefcase, Sam removes his journal with his journal-writing pen clipped to its cover. He puts everything in order on the table (in effect, creating a portable altar), takes a sip of his coffee, a bite of his pie, three slow, deep breaths, and begins to write. In the midst of clattering dishes, yelled orders, the sounds of the El train crashing overhead, and horns honking outside, Sam descends into the peace and quiet of his journal. He tells me that he is transported by this ritual, that it renews his spirit and brings him serenity. "And," he points out, "the middle of my hectic day is when I most need to reconnect with myself and when I'm most glad about the boost I get!" He adds that, for him, the diner is a sanctuary, the table an altar, and the background noise a familiar and somehow comforting refrain.

Sam returns to his office fully refreshed, inspired by the ideas that appeared on his journal pages, and restored with the patience to cope with the crunch of end-of-the-day paperwork and phone calls. During the rush-hour drive home, he mulls over an intriguing insight that emerged as he ate his pie. While helping his wife make dinner and put the kids to bed, he is peaceful and attentive.

Purification

WATER HAS ALWAYS SYM-bolized purification and release. East Indian Hindus view the River Ganges as a sacred source of both functions; Christians all over the world conduct the baptismal rite with holy water; the Japanese rinse their mouths and hands in a fountain before entering the gate of a Shinto shrine. And for centuries, Jewish women have used the *mikva*, a communal bath, in which ritual cleansing takes place.

Often, without realizing that we are engaging in ritualized behavior, we use water to purify ourselves, bathing sleep from our eyes in the morning and the cares of the day from our faces at night. These simple acts are soothing and renewing, a good way to begin times of rest or activity. Creating a conscious ritual when we perform these acts will give them a deeper meaning in our lives.

Intention
To release debilitating influences.

Timing
When you feel overwhelmed by negative thoughts, feelings, or events.

Ingredients
Soap scented with eucalyptus (purification), fresh towel, shower.

Recipe
Consciously approach your shower as an opportunity to let go of worries about your health, relationships, work, finances, or anything else that saps your positive energy. Imagine that the running water gathers all of the stress residue from the pores and crevices of your body, propelling it from the top of your head, over your shoulders and arms, down the length of your body, and out of your life. Allow the physical tension clinging to your muscles to wash away with the emotional stress. Imagine releasing your mind and spirit from all negative influences while you cleanse your body.

As soon as you feel yourself fully renewed, step out of the shower and gently wrap yourself in a warm towel. Stand still for a moment. Then take two or three slow, deep breaths to purify your lungs and signify the completion of the ritual.

RITUAL REALITY

Fifteen-year-old Sally won the lead in her school play. Excited and scared, for weeks she only did her schoolwork and rehearsed her lines. Finally, the big day arrived. Sally awoke with feelings of panic and doom. Her head throbbed and her stomach ached. She wanted to run away.

Her mother took one look at her face and put her arms around Sally. After listening to Sally describe her feelings, her mother mentioned the purification ritual she'd learned in one of my workshops. After listening to the description,

Sally decided she'd give it a try; anything was better than the way she felt!

She went into the bathroom, took off her nightgown, and turned on the shower, carefully adjusting the temperature. She stepped in and felt the water rush over her body. With her eyes closed she began to chant, "I now release all feelings of panic and thoughts of humiliation. I let go of my worries about the play. I wash my insecurities straight down the drain."

As an actress, Sally had no trouble imagining that the water actually released these limiting beliefs from her mind and body. She started to feel calmer and lighter. A sense of her own creativity and strength seemed to fill her whole being. After ten minutes, Sally emerged from the shower and wrapped herself in the warm towel. She knew this wasn't the last time she'd experience stage fright, but at least now she was smiling and confident, ready for her big night.

Basket of Support

WE HAVE ALL EXPERIENCED times when we feel alone in the world, no matter how many loving people surround us. For some reason, many of us believe that we need to overcome difficulties by ourselves. At these moments we view asking for help as a sign of weakness. I call this the Lone Ranger Syndrome. Creating a shield around ourselves feels easier than exposing our weaknesses. The truth is, however, that it's much harder to be vulnerable than to pretend to be tough. It requires true strength to reach out and ask for help.

Meredith Young-Sowers, director of the Stillpoint Institute for Life Healing, created this ritual, and I see it as a way of helping those who suffer from the Lone Ranger Syndrome. A powerful resource, it provides comfort and connection.

Intention

To give and receive support.

Timing

At least once a week, or as needed. Many people use their baskets daily.

Ingredients

Basket, small pieces of paper, pen or pencil.

Recipe

Begin by taking a few minutes to focus on centering in your heart—allowing yourself to feel open and the chatter in your mind to grow silent. Think of something beautiful that makes you happy. Take three deep breaths directly into your heart center (the area between the breast bones), and as the air fills your chest imagine sending love to everyone you care about.

Now think about all of those people, places, animals, or objects that you feel support your efforts and your life. Include those who have passed into Spirit. Write the name of each person on a small piece of paper and place the slips into the basket, which you can keep on your altar. Whenever you do this ritual, choose one name from the basket, and then consciously send and receive love with that person throughout your day.

RITUAL REALITY

Dorothy awoke with feelings of dread about a major presentation she had to give for her foundation. If it went well, the project she had been working on for the last eight months would receive funding; if her presentation was a failure, all of her work would be in vain. Although she had prepared for this day with great care, Dorothy now felt scared and incompetent. Her heart pounded, and she wanted to cry.

As she paced around her bedroom, her eyes lit on the basket of support that she had created in one of my workshops. She walked over to it and picked out a slip of paper. Happily, she drew her college roommate, Karen. Dorothy sat down on her bed and imagined Karen sitting on the other side, smiling. Karen had always been her number-one fan, the first to congratulate her on any success, large or small. Just thinking about her gave Dorothy a renewed sense of courage and confidence.

On an impulse, Dorothy went to the phone and dialed Karen's number. To her surprise, Karen answered and immediately exclaimed, "What a coincidence! Just this morning I took our college yearbook off the shelf and smiled at pictures of us!"

Coincidence? I don't think so. In any case, after Karen's reassurance Dorothy knew that she was not alone and that even if this meeting didn't work out the way she hoped, many more promising opportunities would come her way.

Time and again, I have been amazed when, after choosing a friend's name from my basket, I later discovered that she picked my name from her basket that same day. Other times, I have imagined friends and surrounded them with my love; within a day or two, they have called to say that they had been sick or scared and suddenly felt my presence as a source of comfort.

Bedtime

REMEMBER WHEN YOU WERE a small child and could fall asleep the minute your head hit the pillow? Remember waking up eager for the day, jumping out of bed full of energy and optimism? One of the reasons that children sleep so soundly and wake so easily is because they experience their feelings deeply in the moment and then let them go. As adults, unfortunately many of us tend to mull things over and over. During bedtime we frequently rehash the events of the day—and the emotions that accompanied them. This creates a constant stream of images and conversations that keep us awake and also negatively affect our sleep. You can't talk and sleep at the same time.

This ritual will help you achieve closure from your day and enjoy a calm, peaceful night's rest.

Intention ⁓
To let the day fall into the past.

Timing ⁓
Before you retire for the night.

Ingredients ⁓
Essence of lavender (calmness), spray bottle or diffuser, piece of paper, calming music.

Recipe ⁓
Set aside between five and twenty minutes before going to sleep. Sit comfortably and take a few slow, deep belly breaths (see page 28) to quiet your mind. You may want to play some music softly to set the mood. Write down everything you've accomplished today on a single piece of paper. Or, if you keep a journal, write it there. Even if you've managed only to take a baby step toward a goal, it is important to acknowledge that progress. Learning to recognize your efforts and feel proud of yourself will lead to greater strength and confidence.

Now you're ready for bed. Put a few drops of lavender essence on your pillow and turn out the light. Breathe in the soothing scent and proudly remember what you have learned and accomplished during the day.

RITUAL REALITY

Alan had one of those days when everything seemed to go wrong. First his computer crashed; then Cynthia, his secretary, told him that she was quitting. As if that weren't enough, his wife called to tell him that the washing machine broke and would cost more to fix than to buy a new one. By the time he arrived home, his head throbbed, his eyes burned, and all of his muscles were rigid with tension.

After dinner, Alan tried to relax with a book; then he tried to watch some TV, but nothing caught his interest. Exasperated, he decided to call it a night and go to bed. He tossed and turned for hours, his day flickering in his mind like an old movie. *If only he had saved his report before taking a coffee break. If only he had talked to Cynthia last week when she looked so troubled. If only, if only. . . .*

Finally, out of desperation, he decided to try the ritual his sister, Jamie, had told him about. "Nothing ventured, nothing gained," he thought. Alan went into his den, turned on the CD-player, and put on his favorite disc. After taking a pencil

and a tablet from his desk, he settled himself in his easy chair, took a few very deep breaths, and started to write.

He began with the day's accomplishments, then added a list of the things that had gone wrong and what he had learned from them. Alan realized that by focusing on the negative aspects of events, he had missed the insights or lessons to be gained from each one. For example, while losing Cynthia upset him, now he could find someone with more appropriate qualifications. He decided to give her a going-away party to let her know how much he appreciated her dedication. It made him happy to imagine how much this would mean to her.

Alan reviewed what he had written and realized that he needed to learn how to deal with change and surprise in a more productive way. He decided to sign up for a stress management seminar being offered in the fall. Then he turned off the CD-player and the light, and went to bed musing about the variety of spiritual and practical benefits a simple bedtime ritual could bring.

Follow-Up
Reread these pages regularly, taking pleasure in your achievements.

Chapter Four

RITES OF PASSAGE

HOW MANY PEOPLE DO YOU know who hate change? Try asking Uncle George to switch to another brand of coffee; listen to Rita rant when she reads that her favorite TV show has been canceled; take your own pulse after discovering your dependable, long-term handyman has suddenly moved away. We're all creatures of habit. Even such seemingly minor alterations in our daily existence can throw us, because we simply don't like change. We resist the discombobulation it brings and the stress it leaves in its wake. Ironically, these days change is the only thing we can count on.

Not long ago, most people spent all of their working years with one company, lived their whole lives in the same house, and practiced their religion—and its rituals—with unquestioning regularity. Now the words *job security* often seem like a contradiction in terms, and the "family home" might crisscross the continent more than a few times. Children move away from parents, and grandparents move to retirement communities.

We have become nomads, focused on our own small clans and concerns, isolated from our far-flung extended families and traditions. We no longer have a sense of community and its once recurring—and therefore predictable—events. In the process we have lost touch with a sense of connection and with the rituals that once made life seem coherent and complete. When change happens, it blindsides us; one change triggers others, and suddenly it feels as if every aspect of our lives is off-kilter.

Rituals of transition can help us segue from one circumstance to another, one year to the next, and one life stage to another. They provide perspective, clarity, and a sense of purpose, while at the same time they calm the physical and emotional upheavals that accompany change.

These rites of passage will transform your view. Instead of seeing change as a nasty trick of fate, you'll recognize it as a valuable gift, moving you away from feelings of alienation and toward an understanding that your life is part of a grander scheme.

The New Year

EVERY CULTURE IN THE world celebrates the advent of a new year as a fresh beginning. Watch your head in an Italian town on New Year's Eve, because the inhabitants literally *do* "out with the old" by throwing unwanted possessions from their windows. Everything that lands on the pavement is up for grabs, making "street shopping" a fun part of the night's activity. The Chinese have more moderate customs that include paying their debts and sweeping their floors to prepare for the new year. During *Tashlich,* the Hebrew ritual for Rosh Hashanah ("new year"), Jews write their sins on tiny scraps of paper and then cast the previous year's transgressions into a body of water. Many Eastern European families sing special songs as children scatter grain around their houses with the hope that prosperity will follow. Closer to home, my client Roberta spends every January first cleaning out her closets, packing up all of the unwanted items, and driving them to a shelter for battered women. Another client, Jack, has an annual New Year's Day football extravaganza at his apartment; while at a glance it looks like a tribute to testosterone, in fact, it renews important bonds among old friends, all of whom have told Jack how much this time together means to them.

The Bulgarian master Omraam Mikhaël Aïvanhov taught me that each of the first twelve days in January represents one month of the coming year. In other words, the first day stands for January, the second for February, and so on. This belief imbues these twelve days with great power and provides an amazing chance to think about how you want your upcoming year to go. By practicing loving kindness, openness, and generosity, while giving thoughtful attention to the significance of each day, you will consecrate the coming year.

Intention

To create a *vision collage* that expresses your resolutions.

Timing

Within the first twelve days of the new year.

Ingredients

Sage (purification) yellow candle (manifestation) chocolate or honey (sweetness), poster board, glue, scissors, old magazines, music.

R e c i p e 〜

After you've assembled the ingredients, sit quietly for a few minutes and breathe deeply as you reflect on the year that has just drawn to a close. Think about the people that mattered most to you, your greatest accomplishments, challenging difficulties, and the lessons you learned. Don't get stuck in *might-have-beens* or self-recrimination. Keep moving through the year with your mind's eye on the larger perspective. Recognize the patterns in your life that keep you stuck. Are you resisting exercise, even as you endlessly complain about that extra twenty pounds? Are you always short of money, but not taking the time to balance your checkbook? Explore your fears—the feelings that keep you from your own joyous nature. Write down the limiting beliefs or habits that you wish to leave behind with the old year. Now burn the paper. As the paper burns, be aware that you have just made space for new ideas, people, and opportunities to enter your life. Wash your hands in sage water or burn sage and inhale its cleansing aroma.

Take out the magazines and before leafing through them, ask yourself "What brings me joy?" It seems strange to think how infrequently we ask—or answer—this question. As you pick up your scissors, make a conscious decision to let your spirit, not your reason, guide you; when you allow your heart to make choices, you'll move into closer alignment with your soul.

Start cutting out pictures of anything that you want to manifest in your life during the coming year—general images that evoke peace, clarity, and happiness as well as more specific ones. For example, if exercising is a goal, choose a photo of someone engaged in an activity you think might be fun for you; if you'd like to travel, look for pictures of intriguing places. Keep searching and snipping until you've accumulated a sizeable stack of wishes and dreams. Finally, fill out a deposit slip to yourself in the amount of money you'd like to bring into your life in the coming year.

Before you start pasting pictures, fill your room with music—anything you love—that will add more joy to making your collage. Close your eyes for a moment and recall the fun you had as a small child cutting, pasting, and arranging. Let that fully remembered happiness fill your head and animate your hands as you work.

When you've finished, prop up your collage in a place where you'll see it every day. Put a yellow candle on your altar and light it. Let your eyes roam over the pictures you've collected, stopping here and there to focus on the meaning of what you see. Looking at these images will energize them, giving them a real presence in your life. End the ritual by tasting some chocolate, a spoonful of honey, or anything that will imbue the coming year with sweetness.

RITUAL REALITY

Every year for over a decade I've led a vision workshop in early January for a group of men and women, many of whom come every year. Sitting in a circle, we start by passing around a bowl of spring water sprinkled with the essence of sage, in which we wash our hands to purify ourselves and sanctify the space.

After I lead a guided meditation to center us and open our hearts, each participant shares important moments from the past year. Some report that many of the visions they included on the previous year's collage had, in fact, materialized. For example, in 1996 I was drawn to a picture of the Hawaiian goddess Pele, and without knowing why, I put her in the center of my collage. Six months later I found myself in a helicopter, watching in awe and fascination as Pele's volcano, Kilauea, spewed flaming lava!

Before we start our collages, I conduct a burning ritual to release old limiting beliefs and habits. The workshop runs all day, filled with laugh-ter, conversation, and a lot of activity as we create our masterworks. When we've finished, we clean up the room and then sit in our circle, proudly displaying our collages. Each is as unique as its maker: one is bold and assertive; another reflects spirituality; others express humor, a wish for serenity, or a desire for companionship. All of the participants talk about their visions, sharing their hopes, insights, and surprises. For example, Jody initially thought she was going to focus on her career, but instead her collage spoke of nature and home.

We listen to each other carefully, and I remind everyone also to listen to themselves carefully whenever they review their vision collage during the next twelve months. We say our good-byes, punctuated with joyful wishes for the new year, each of us filled with warmth and optimism.

Follow-Up

During the new year, look at your vision collage regularly, allowing it to nestle deeper and deeper into your unconscious. Share it with family and friends to enhance its significance in your daily life.

A New Home

VIRTUALLY EVERY CULTURE has a traditional ceremony to celebrate and bless a new home. On Malta, a priest prays inside a new house for seven days before the newlyweds are allowed to move in. Every day, as a way to take part in the sanctification process, family members bring food to the holy man. For centuries, Russians have swept their new homes with rock salt, which they believe releases negative vibrations. After they finish, they ring a bell to usher in a benign spiritual presence. American settlers came together to help raise the roof of a new home, expressing their welcome and best wishes for safety and security. The Amish still do this. Norse pagan rituals included bringing a living tree into the home in the middle of winter, believing that it held the earth spirit, which would fill the rooms with its blessing—a precursor, of course, to the Christmas tree. And for hundreds of years, Jews the world over have placed a *mezuzah* (a small cylindrical case containing a scroll of Torah verses) outside the door of a new home. Every time anyone enters or leaves, the person touches it and recites a prayer: "May God protect my going out and coming in, now and forever."

Much of modern Western society has replaced these rituals with housewarming parties and presents. In the process, the spiritual aspects have all but disappeared. However, a ritual blessing will last longer than the lava lamp from your fraternity brother, and I predict it will far more powerfully illuminate your perception and experience of *home*.

This ritual is designed to sanctify your new space, whether it be a cabin in the woods, a studio apartment, or a Tudor mansion.

Intention
To clear your new space of old influences and infuse it with your own meaning.

Timing
Immediately before or after your move-in day.

Ingredients
Spring water, salt (purification), bread (nourishment), honey (sweetness), purple candle (spirituality), rose (love), plant (nature), altar cloth.

Recipe ⌒

First, clean your new space; mop the floors, dust the windowsills, and scrub all of the appliances. Then take a bath, sprinkling a pinch of salt into the water to release any negative energy that you absorbed while cleaning. This salt bath serves a dual purpose—purifying both your body and your soul.

After you get dressed, pour salt into a small bowl and circle the outside of your home, spreading a thin line of salt as you walk. If you are moving into an apartment, scatter a few grains over your entrance threshold. As the salt settles, ask that your space be protected and blessed. Continue this process once you are back inside, sprinkling salt in every corner of every room, in all of the closets and cupboards. And as you walk about, repeat words that you feel will banish unwanted energy; for example, "I clear this space so that I may live here in peace and harmony." If you prefer, you also can clear the space by lighting sage, sage/cedar, or by using other combinations of scents (see Chapter Two), or performing a physical act, such as clapping.

After you've cleared your rooms, return to each one, blessing it and setting the intention for its use. Bless your bedroom for bringing you peaceful sleep, romantic encounters, or hoped-for fertility. Bless the kitchen for providing space for nourishment, the bathroom for release and cleansing, your office as a place to work and be creative, and your living room for welcoming friends and family.

Now create an altar. Light a candle to evoke the spirit of safety and love, and place the rose beside it, symbolizing the love that you wish to bring into your new home. The bread ensures dependable nourishment, the honey promises sweetness, and a plant will align you with nature's goodness. If you are religious you might include an item from your faith to represent God's blessing in your new home.

RITUAL REALITIES

House blessings are very individual. Think of your intention and refer to Chapter Two to figure out which tools and symbols best convey what you would like *your* house blessing to express. Or maybe you want to borrow from either of the examples below.

✐ Ed and Michelle, a couple in their late fifties, had just celebrated their twenty-fifth anniversary by buying their first home. Apartment dwellers all of their adult lives, they were excited *and* daunted by the prospect of this new responsibility. They asked for my help in designing a ritual to mark this event, as well as to provide spiritual support.

We worked together, integrating what they knew about each other with all that they hoped for in their new house. A date was chosen for the ceremony and the couple happily set about cleaning all of the rooms, cupboards and closets, and the yard and garage to get ready.

Sunrise was their favorite time of day—a happy coincidence because many cultures believe that the first rays of the sun have the greatest life force, or *mana*; they decided to begin the ritual at dawn. The day arrived. Michelle and Ed drove into their new driveway just as the sun began to illuminate the sky and they saw their house bathed in soft light as they walked up the front steps. After placing a welcome mat at the front door, they sprinkled salt on the threshold and entered their new house. Since they had chosen part of a Balinese ritual that I learned from feng-shui master Alex Stark, they then carried a bowl of smoldering white sage into every room to clean the energy of the whole house. They greeted each space, introduced themselves, said a few words about their hopes and dreams, and then, setting the bowl on the floor, they clapped their hands.

Later, they told me that they initially felt a little self-conscious. But recalling the Balinese belief that forceful clapping has the power to break down stagnant energy left by previous inhabitants, the couple's clapping developed a real resonance.

Before leaving each room, they rang the small brass Balinese bell I had given them, promising that its tone would bring harmony to the air.

When they finished the ritual, Ed and Michelle returned to their bedroom, where they lit a white candle. They spoke about the ritual's meaning for their new home and their new life in it. Then they shared the breakfast picnic they had prepared to symbolize the physical and spiritual nourishment that their house offered them.

Elliott and Phyllis began their house blessing by sprinkling cornmeal (abundance of harvest) around the grounds. They honored the land for giving them a solid foundation for their new home. In a shaded spot near their front porch, they dug a hole in the earth and buried money (prosperity) and a tourmaline crystal (healing and balance).

The couple then lit a smudge stick of sage and sweetgrass and walked around every room purifying and sanctifying the space. Elliott and Phyllis also built an altar of protection for their home by placing their favorite fluorite crystal—to release unwanted energy from the premises—next to the hanging wind chimes they had purchased while traveling in the Southwest. The chimes held personal meaning for the couple because they had bought them with the express purpose of hanging them in a new home, even though at the time, they hadn't found the house of their dreams. When they returned from Santa Fe to the East Coast where they lived, one of the messages on their answering machine was from a realtor, informing them that the house they had their eye on before was now available—a previously signed deal had fallen through. Elliott and Phyllis were sure that the new chimes had brought them good luck.

To complete this blessing, their friends and new neighbors joined them in a wonderful gathering that not only celebrated their new home but their Syrian Jewish heritage as well. Phyllis asked both their mothers to take part. Gloria, Phyllis's mom, brought the couple a beautifully decorated basket containing the traditional house blessing ingredients—dried yeast (nourishment), oil (prosperity), a bible (spirituality) and small seeds (good luck), which they placed in the corners of each room. And Elliott's mother, Pauline, brought a feast of Sephardic delights for all to share. Everyone agreed that there could be no better way to bless a new home than with food— *the* symbol of nurturing—that everyone loves.

Celebrating Birthdays

ICE CREAM AND CAKE, GIFTS and games, making wishes and blowing out candles. Is this how you remember your childhood birthdays? Is it very different from the way you celebrated last year? We all tend to hold on to these traditions because they let us experience the passage of time—at least for the moment—the way we did when we were kids. Often it's as if a cultural taboo keeps us from honoring our growing maturity and enjoying the gains we have made, thanks to the accumulating years.

In fact, our birthdays should be viewed through a three-way lens—the first focusing on the rich lessons of the past, the second on the opportunities and rewards of the present, and the third providing a glimpse of the surprises and wisdom awaiting us in the future. This ritual will enable you to see the full picture through a clear lens. From this perspective, you'll see yourself moving along a path that spirals upward toward growth and fulfillment, instead of fixating on the past or stagnating in the present.

Intention ～
To honor your life journey.

Timing ～
On the eve or day of your birthday.

Ingredients ～
Bath or shower (purification), white clothing (purity), object or picture to discard, four candles—purple (spirituality), green (healing), blue (clarity), and yellow (vision), your favorite incense, sage or copal (to strengthen purification).

Recipe ～
Begin by bathing and dressing in white to signify the purification of your body and spirit. On your altar, light the purple candle and burn one of the herbs to cleanse the space around you. Breathe deeply and take a few minutes to settle into the sense of timelessness you've created. Now light the green candle in honor of the gift of life given to you by your parents. Thank them for this—

your first, and most important, birthday present. Create a balanced memory of their influence, with the good intentions and acts resting beside the conflicts and difficulties. Recognize that both aspects nurtured your growth. Next, light the blue candle in honor of the past year. Review the lessons learned and those that you might still be struggling with. Take the object or picture you've chosen to discard; consider its past meaning in your life, as well as the significance of its absence in your future. Bless it and let it go. Light the yellow candle to illuminate your vision for the next year. Many native cultures believe that birthdays are the most powerful times to communicate with Spirit, to express your dreams and to petition for your hopes. Be sure to include your willingness to work with Spirit to achieve your goals.

RITUAL REALITY

For her twenty-first birthday, Vanessa sent invitations to everyone, friends and family, who mattered to her. She took two vacation days from work and spent them cleaning her apartment, cooking, and creating an altar at one end of her living room. She decorated it with beautiful flowers and old photographs that chronicled her childhood, including one of her as an infant in a pale-yellow wool sweater, sitting on her mother's lap. Beside it, she placed the same sweater, which she had found in an attic trunk the previous summer. Whenever she looked at it, she recalled her mother's story of making the tiny garment while she was pregnant with Vanessa, knitting loving dreams for her baby into each row.

When her guests arrived, Vanessa had them stand in a semicircle around the altar, and then took her mother's hand and led her to a chair right beside it. For nearly an hour, Vanessa reviewed the important moments in her life and the major role her mother played in each one. She then presented her mother with a beautifully wrapped package. Inside, her mother found an album of photos matching those on the altar. Under each one, Vanessa had written the memories and emotions she had just shared. Because her mother was as much a celebrant in her "birth" day, Vanessa led the guests in singing "Happy Birthday" to her mom. Now Vanessa felt that she could take her place in society as an adult, and that this ritual set the intention for the next phase of her life.

Retirement

REMEMBER JAMMING A year's worth of fun and relaxation into only two weeks of vacation? What about all of the conversations that began, "*Oh, boy! When I retire, I'm gonna . . .*"? Suddenly, you have fifty-two weeks of vacation; you can do all of those things you've wanted to do for years. Your family is busy making plans, and your friends envy your new freedom. You know that it's a time to reflect proudly on your career and celebrate its completion. So why does your heart feel heavy with grief? *Why do you feel so low?*

The answer to that question isn't so simple. There are many explanations why the first few months or even year after retiring can be a time of sadness and confusion. First and foremost, it is a period of separation—from colleagues, from a familiar routine, and even from your own identity as a worker.

It's time for you to decode all of these emotions. Only by reviewing and ordering the meanings of the past can you open your heart to the possibilities of the present and future. This ritual provides a way to structure this process by looking at *yourself* in the moment, the paths you've taken to get here, and those you hope to follow in the years ahead.

Intention

To acknowledge the accomplishments, friends, and lessons from your past career and to open your heart to future ones.

Timing

Your last day of work or soon after.

Ingredients

Copal (purification), purple candle (spiritual inspiration), yellow candle (new beginnings), soothing music, photograph or object from your work life, glue, small box, pencil and stack of paper, young plant (continuity), new pot, potting soil, charcoal, small fireproof bowl.

Recipe

Place the ingredients on your altar. Start the music and light the purple candle. Burn the copal on the charcoal and sit quietly for a minute or two, breathing deeply to cleanse your spirit and fill your body with new energy. Now place the photo or object in the center of a piece of paper and write all of the words that come to mind when you think about your working years—co-workers' names, deals you made, people you taught or mentored, the brand of shoes you wore or the computer you used, as well as important events. After you've filled one sheet of paper, start another. When you're finished, read what you've written and experience the emotions that accompany each entry. You may feel like sharing some of these feelings with one or two people you recalled. On a separate piece of paper, make a list of people to write or telephone over the next few days. Now put all of these pages (except the list) into the box.

Move the young plant, the new pot, and the soil to the center of your altar. Repot the plant, being aware of your own move from one environment to another. Think about your own situation as one in which you, too, are young and in need of special care, and about ways to nurture your own growth as you will this plant. Wash and dry the discarded pot and place it in the box. Clean up the table and sit quietly, again breathing deeply for a few minutes. Then extinguish the purple candle, releasing the past, and light the yellow one as an expression of eagerness to grow into your new life.

RITUAL REALITY

After thirty years directing a government agency, my longtime friend Nancy announced her retirement. Although she had always loved her job, she now felt that it kept her from the freedom she needed to explore her creativity. Excited as she was with her decision, she also felt overcome with feelings of sadness and anxiety. She asked me to help her create a ritual that offered a sense of comfort and closure while preparing her for the next phase of her life.

I carefully considered what I knew about Nancy's past and all I could imagine for her future. Then I invited her to my home, asking her to bring an item or two from the office that she might be willing to part with. At the appointed time, Nancy arrived with an organizational chart she designed a few years earlier and a coffee mug her mentor had given her when she first started working.

We sat together at my dining room table, now an altar covered with a blue cloth to enhance communication. Nancy lit the gold candle (evoking courage) that I had placed to one side, then the sage leaves (purification), resting in a white bowl. After I explained the meanings of the colors and herb I had chosen, we sat quietly for a couple of minutes, breathing the aroma of sage and allowing it to cleanse our spirits and sanctify the air around us. Then I asked her to talk about her career, saying whatever came to mind. She spoke about people, hard lessons, valued rewards, and her amazing progress through the maze of red tape that defines governmental agencies. She laughed and cried as she imagined thirty years of memories.

Finally, I asked her to explain the origins and purpose of the organizational chart. She quickly grasped that it was a metaphor for her career and nodded that yes, she was ready to release it. She crumpled the chart, threw it into a metal pail on the floor, and ignited it. As the paper burst into flames, her tears signaled her acceptance of the end of this time in her life. Then she handed me the mug, expecting that it would be broken or otherwise disposed of. Instead, I reached under the table and pulled out a few cuttings from my begonia, and a small bag of soil. Joyfully, she planted the stems in the mug, acknowledging that her future would indeed grow out of the foundation of her past. She mused about her hopes and dreams, anticipating the journey ahead without anxiety. We sprinkled the ashes of the organizational chart over the soil to represent the nourishment provided by the past, and added rose water to symbolize her commitment to nurture herself.

Follow-Up
Write or call the people on your list.

Becoming an Elder

FOR THOUSANDS OF YEARS, cultures around the world have valued the knowledge and insight provided by their parents, grandparents, aunts, and uncles. They have perceived aging as a natural and venerable process, supported by the younger generations' respect for their elders. Hawaiians believe that wisdom comes only in the eightieth year, at which time they hold a great celebration. Older Native Americans consider it a sign of respect to be addressed as "Grandmother" or "Grandfather."

We, on the other hand, worship youth. Our society ignores the important stories of our elders, and dismisses the wisdom of experience they have to offer, because of our own fear of aging—the chosen rite of passage for *our* aging family members is the move to a nursing home.

The time has come to appreciate the value of elderhood. We can make a commitment to honor and celebrate those who are older, to turn the aging process into a sacred event in which we all participate. Families and friends can create a sense of tribal unity, with each of us benefitting from the stories and wisdom of our elders.

Intention

To sanctify and rejoice in a loved one's advancing years.

Timing

On the day marking the seventy-fifth (or later) birthday of a loved one.

Ingredients

Photographs, memorabilia, gold candle (masculinity and the sun) or silver candle (femininity and the moon), favorite music and foods, recorder and tapes, meaningful gifts.

Recipe

Fashion an invitation that explains the purpose of this gathering and how it will differ from an ordinary birthday celebration; send it to family and friends, including children. Ask someone to run the audio- or videotape equipment. Make a list of topics for the honoree to speak about—the most important events and people from each decade, the lessons learned, descriptions of childhood clothing and food, and the means of transportation and communication during each era.

On the day of the event, create an altar holding photos and important objects from the honoree's life. When everybody has gathered, light the candle and seat all of the guests in a circle. Indulge in the pleasure of storytelling and recapture the rich, multicultural tradition of honoring your grandparents' heritage. Then, ask your questions. While keeping to a realistic schedule, encourage the elder to reminisce; lead others in expressions of appreciation for each memory and anecdote.

Serve the meal, and while you eat invite everyone to share what they have gained by knowing the guest of honor. Before bringing out the dessert, present the gifts. They can be handmade, traditional, or inventive—a facial for your great-aunt, a massage for your grandfather, season tickets for the ballet or baseball team. Ask the youngest member of the family to present the gifts as a way of connecting past, present, and future generations. End the ritual with the elder's favorite music and dessert.

RITUAL REALITY

Nora wanted to mark her father Marty's eightieth birthday with a ritual that would express her love and respect for him. They had always been close, but had become even closer since her mother's death five years earlier. Father and daughter sat down one evening to make a guest list and design invitations. They invited twenty-one people, mostly family members and friends of Nora and her two brothers who had grown up with their dad's everready smile and gentle advice. Only a few of his own friends would be able to attend.

As Nora described the birthday ritual she imagined, and Marty's role in its preparation and enactment, his enthusiasm increased. He pulled out photos and items he wanted to share with the guests. As memories poured out, Nora realized that she had never asked him many important questions. Her dad continued talking while Nora designed the invitation. For the cover, she chose a picture of Marty as a lanky teenager standing beside his uncle's brand-new Packard sedan. Inside she wrote that the party would honor the breadth of Marty's experience and wisdom. Each guest would be blessed by his stories, and in return, would be asked to bring at least one "Marty story" of their own.

The birthday ritual was a huge success. Everyone, young and old alike, loved the altar Marty had created with the photos and memorabilia he'd chosen to display. They sat engrossed as he told his stories and later were rewarded by the sweet expressions on his face when they, in turn, recounted tale after tale of his wisdom and understanding.

Bill and his twin brother, Tom, who grew up next door to Nora, recalled Marty coaching them when they wanted to make the junior-high football team. "We were these two scrawny kids, completely uncoordinated and clueless. Marty taught us the rules of the game and the importance of teamwork." Bill smiled as Tom added, "That's really what got us on the team and kept us there through high school. We were always the scrawniest, but boy did we know our stuff! Our coach said we had the best team spirit he'd ever seen. Marty taught us that."

Esther, a large, shy woman who had gone to school with Nora and still had the same thir-teen-year-old baby face, remembered when Marty taught her to dance. "Jerry Parker had asked me to the sock hop, and I was so thrilled I said yes, and then panicked. Marty was the only grown-up who noticed that something was bothering me. When I told him what was going on, he had Nora come into the kitchen, turned on the radio, and the three of us danced. By the time Jerry and I got to the hop I felt like I could really boogie!"

As the guests left, they expressed their gratitude to Nora and Marty for reminding them of all the reasons to honor the elders of the community.

Follow-Up
Give a copy of the tape to the honored elder. Listen to or watch it together at least twice during the coming year, reminiscing about the ritual itself.

Chapter Five

RITUALS FOR MOVING
THROUGH STRESSFUL TIMES

We ALL KNOW THAT NOTHING stays the same. Life is a dynamic and complex interplay of ever-changing forces. Yet, when there is a shift in our circumstances—an unexpected reversal at work or a sudden transformation in a relationship—many of us panic. We are over-taken by feelings of hopelessness or helplessness.

For thousands of years, people all over the world have enacted sacred ceremonies that honor and maintain harmony between human beings and life's uncertainties. These simple rites support the belief that a good relationship with Spirit strengthens our ability to accept whatever life brings, which ultimately gives us peace. Staying centered in the midst of upheaval is even more of a daunting challenge in today's world.

Ritual can help you rescue and comfort yourself during times of spiritual and emotional turmoil. This chapter offers you a series of simple rites to help change your perception of and reaction to stressful events. These rituals will give you insight into the root of your anxiety, strengthen your tol-erance for stress, and help you develop new coping skills to diminish your feelings of helplessness.

We obviously can't avoid stress—it goes with the territory of life—but we *can* modify the way we respond to taxing situations and change the lens through which we view them. It might sur-prise you to discover that being fired from a job can be a blessing. Or that a partner's unexpected demand might lead to growth and enhanced inti-may, no matter how earth-shattering the change feels at first. During such stress-inducing chal-lenges and changes in everyday life you need to take time to look at your fears and meet them head-on, to feel your feelings, and to truly process the change.

These simple rituals will help you do just that. Eventually you will welcome whatever comes your way for the unexpected gifts that come with it. And you will see how important it is to embrace change and to understand that pieces of life naturally come together, fall apart, and come together again in new, even positive ways.

The Fear Box

YOU'RE IN A PANIC: **Y**OU just can't understand the new computer system at work and everything you do at the office depends on it; your bank account is nearly empty and it's only the middle of the month; the man or woman of your dreams has just asked you on a date and you feel as if your entire future is at stake. What do all of these situations have in common? Whether they have the potential for enormous happiness or disaster, each inspires anxiety.

Many cultures present their fears to God through prayer or offerings of flowers, incense, and foods. According to the Kabbalah, the mystical center of Judaism, you must acknowledge your deepest vulnerabilities and hand them over to God before you can truly know who you are.

This simple ritual will help stop that sinking feeling in your stomach. It will give you a place to put those feelings of anxiety before they become so powerful that they inhibit you from thinking rationally or from taking constructive action toward resolving your fears.

Intention

To release feelings of anxiety and expectations of doom.

Timing

Every time you experience fearful thoughts.

Ingredients

Essence of frankincense (to release fear) and lavender (calming), multifaceted piece of clear quartz (to break up negative energy), small cardboard box, black marker, crayon, or paint, pencil and paper.

Recipe

Start by placing a few drops of frankincense in a bowl of warm water and inhale the calming aroma. Cover a shoe box or other small container with black paint, marker, or crayon (black represents fear and the weight it adds to your life). Whenever you have an anxious thought, write it down on a slip of paper and put it in the box. You can be very specific: "I'm scared I'll make a fool of myself at this meeting." Or you can be more general: "I'm getting old, unattractive, and forgetful."

Don't judge what you write, it doesn't matter if someone else would find it stupid or silly. Be honest with yourself; honesty leads to clarity and can produce positive action. Set the quartz crystal next to the box to help absorb the negative energy.

If you are away from home when these thoughts strike, write them down anyway and put the piece of paper in a pocket and out of your mind, confident that you'll be able to drop it into your fear box as soon as you get home. Just before turning out the lights at bedtime, finish the ritual by emptying the box the way you would empty the trash—an ordinary way to get rid of what you don't want or need. Now turn out the lights. Place a few drops of lavender oil on your pillow to soothe your spirit and lull you to sleep.

RITUAL REALITY

David was fifty years old and beset with worry. He used to think that this stage of his life would be easier than his younger years, when he was adjusting to the demands of marriage, starting a family, and establishing a career. Instead, he now felt overwhelmed by anxiety. He'd read about the "sandwich generation," caught between aging parents and struggling children, and suddenly here he was—smack-dab in the middle of a familial Big Mac. His always healthy father had just been diagnosed with Alzheimer's disease and his mother was panicked. In his own home, his daughter, Jenny, was paralyzed by the prospect of writing college applications and his fourteen-year-old son, Gavin, had been suspended from school for repeated bouts of fighting. David's wife, Beth, was at her wit's end, trying to help the children while also taking care of everything David had always done before his father got sick. Worst of all, she worried about David, who was becoming increasingly anxious, having palpitations, losing weight, and having trouble sleeping.

Finally one morning, Beth hid his car keys. "I've already called your boss," she said as she served him his favorite breakfast. "You're taking a personal day. Now eat while I tell you about something that could help you." Ignoring David's skeptical expression, she described the fear box ritual and then reached into the broom closet and pulled out an old shoe box, painted black. "You might as well try it, honey, 'cause you're not getting your keys back until tomorrow."

In the quiet of his study, David wrote and wrote, one fear per page. He was surprised by some of them—an image of Gavin in reform school, Jenny as an uneducated shop clerk, Beth in love with someone else, and himself alone in a nursing home, suffering from inherited Alzheimer's. The box was full by the time Beth brought in lunch. They spent the afternoon together, talking about David's anxieties—those with and without solutions. He began to realize that while he had some very real problems, the biggest was his own attitude. His surrender to anxiety kept him from being able to discriminate between the things he could change and the things he couldn't, between real threats and those he only imagined. David thanked Beth and then, smiling, he asked for one more favor: "Will you please give me the car keys so I can take you out to dinner?"

Follow-Up

Keep your fear box in a visible place. Use it as an emotional garbage can. Replace what you throw away with positive thoughts, such as "My life is becoming easier." Once a month, clean the crystal with spring water (to release the negative energy that it has absorbed) and place it in the sun to dry.

Moving Through Depression

SOMETIMES DEPRESSION IS an appropriate, even healing response to a major event—the death of a loved one, the loss of a good job, the end of a long-term relationship. While the darkness that follows such events is difficult, the quiet and isolation that surrounds it can be restorative. And because its origins are understandable, friends and family are more likely to be patient and supportive, creating a healing environment.

At other times, simple, everyday events can lead to a depression that seems as difficult to describe as to heal. You might wake up one morning overwhelmed for no apparent reason. This spiritual malaise might last for a day or two, or for months on end. You don't understand it and neither do those around you. Feeling helpless and frustrated, they avoid you, leaving you even more isolated and depressed. At such times, we have a tendency to reach for whatever we think will make us feel better in the moment—eating, shopping, drugs, alcohol, cigarettes—but this leaves us even more alone in the end.*

While studying with a *rimpoche*, a Tibetan Buddhist master, I learned that his tradition believes that sitting still, solitary, and silent only magnifies despair; the best way to release your spirit from depression's grasp is through movement and sound, which have the power to pull you out of the heaviness you're experiencing. They increase the flow of life energy through your body, literally freeing and lifting your spirit. Tai chi and other Eastern disciplines have worked with this principal for centuries.

If we do not express the emotions that cause our depression, we run the risk of an even more serious illness. This ritual uses movement and sound to release debilitating feelings. You can use it as a compass to help you find your way out of despair.

* Major depression should be dealt with by a professional counselor or doctor. This ritual is not meant to supplant professional help.

To release yourself from a pattern of depression and apathy.

Timing ⌒

When you are ready to break through your destructive patterns of dealing with depression arising from everyday concerns.

Ingredients ⌒

Shower, scented candle or essence of vanilla (joy) or jasmine (clears obstacles), percussion instrument (a kitchen pot and wooden spoon will do), dance music, open space, something bright to wear (shirt, scarf, hat), red candle (passion and energy), spring water (purification). Optional: citrus fruit (joy).

Recipe ⌒

Begin by showering and washing your hair. Imagine that the water is cleansing your emotions, as well as your body. (Remember the song from *South Pacific*—"I'm Going to Wash That Man Right out of My Hair"? These lyrics express the symbolic use of shampoo as a means of release.) After dressing in bright colors, bring the essence of vanilla into the air of your room by lighting a scented candle or simply adding extract to a bowl of warm water. Inhale deeply; aromatherapy has been shown to change our physiological and psychological states. The scent of vanilla is one of the best remedies for depression—as are jasmine and citrus. If you don't have vanilla, cut an orange or grapefruit onto a plate and breathe its aroma. Light a red candle and play music that makes you want to dance—it can be rock, rap, hip-hop, or a John Phillip Sousa march—whatever gets you moving.

Now take up your percussion instruments and *make noise*! Find the beat and go with it, first with your hands, then your feet, and then your whole body. MOVE, SING, SHOUT, DANCE, JUMP! This ritual is not about technique or talent; it is about moving through feelings. Lose track of your mind and feel your body. Shout "NO!" to negativity. Allow your depression to flow out with the music. Dance until you feel *exhausted*. Drink some spring water to complete the purification. Turn down the music's volume, but keep it playing for a while as you relax. You'll find that it makes you smile and that as tired as you are, your foot is still tapping in time to the rhythm.

RITUAL REALITY

A college senior, Peter felt depressed and anxious—trapped in his dorm room, buried under textbooks, restricted by term paper deadlines, and facing not only final exams but the future looming ahead. He seriously needed a break, but he didn't feel like going out drinking with the guys for the millionth time. He loved the loud music, dancing, and yelling that characterized those evenings at Phil's Pub, but he hated the smell of sweat, booze, and stale smoke as much as the next morning's hangover.

Suddenly, he had an inspiration. He gathered up a bunch of tapes and his Walkman, found a towel under his bed, glanced one last time at the books on his desk, and walked out of his room, slamming the door as hard as he could. Twenty minutes later, he parked his car on a low bluff overlooking the Pacific. The sun was setting, the wind was gusting, and the air was crisp and clean. He grabbed his gear and skidded down the narrow path to the rocky beach where he dropped his towel and loaded a Snoop Doggie Dog tape into the Walkman. Feeling hidden by the dusky light, Peter began to dance. He grunted to the beat of the rap and his body's exertions, and then he began to make up his own lyrics, punctuating teachers' names and research topics with loud shouts of "NO!" He picked up a couple of rocks and banged them in time to the music. Finally exhausted, Peter stretched out on the shore. It was growing dark and the moon was hidden by thick clouds. He turned off the Walkman and listened to the sound of the waves breaking until he felt ready to leave.

Back at his dorm, Peter was amazed by how unburdened he felt—no longer anxious or depressed. His spirit was free and his body still tingled from dancing in the sea air. No clogged lungs or aching head from hours at Phil's Pub; he felt invigorated and ready to tackle his work.

Follow - Up

From now on, keep essence of vanilla in your bedroom to boost your spirits and remind you of the joy and power you experienced. Whenever you feel low, wear bright colors to energize your body and your spirit. Keep your drum or rattle handy; when the going gets tough, reach for it instead of a cup of coffee or a drink.

Releasing Negativity

YOUR LONG-TERM RELATION-
ship ends with a bang and you spend months
reviewing the scene, castigating yourself with *if
onlys*. You hear that your company is downsizing
to the tune of one hundred jobs and you arrive at
work every morning expecting to find a pink slip
on your desk. You're in your mid-thirties and
every time your mother calls, you immediately
turn into a six-year-old. What's going on? Why do
you always leap to a negative—rather than a positive or even neutral—point of view?

You can probably add hundreds of examples to those listed above—thoughts that result
in your writhing with regret, anxiety, resent-
ment, or anger. These emotions block your
creative juices, inhibit spontaneity, and can make
you prone to physical illness. Native Americans
call them "power drains" because they sap your
energy, leaving you with diminished strength in
your life. This ritual is designed to change how
you respond to negative situations and help you
find constructive ways to deal with them.

Intention ⌒

To release thoughts and feelings of negativity.

Timing ⌒

When you recognize a draining situation.

Ingredients ⌒

Purple candle (spirituality), sandalwood (for centering yourself), matches, paper and pen, fireproof
bowl with sand, small stone, essence of rosemary
(uplifting). Optional: musical instrument (for
release of energy).

Recipe ⌒

You will need about an hour of undisturbed time.
Begin by lighting a purple candle to enhance communication with yourself as well as with others.
Burn sandalwood to help clear your emotions.
Then close your eyes and breathe deeply into
your belly until you feel yourself reaching a state
of relaxation (see page 28). Evoke peaceful memories, such as a lovely garden in bloom or the face

of someone who loves you, or call forth inspiring religious figures such as Isis, the Virgin Mary, or Kuan Yin.

Place your hand over your heart center and imagine that you have access to compassion—the ability to be tender with yourself as well as with others. Be open to accepting all of yourself, even those parts that you don't like. Imagine that each breath you take carries compassion to your spirit. Ask for help in recognizing the negative emotions that steal your energy. It may help to imagine that you are talking to a wise elder, a favorite teacher, or a spiritual guide. Open your eyes and, leaving the rest of the page blank for the moment, write each of the following headings on one side of the paper: *I regret*_____. *I resent*_____. *I fear*_____. *I am angry at*_____. Now start filling in the blanks, allowing the words to flow without judgment. Write until you feel empty.

When you're finished, breathe deeply for a minute or two and then read the list out loud. Read to your pet or to a plant, read to your reflection in a mirror or to a framed photo on your dresser. Your "audience" doesn't matter, but speaking aloud does, because it brings the words—symbolically and literally—into the open. At the end, say "I am now ready to release these negative thoughts and emotions."

In a safe area of your home, burn the paper in the sand-filled bowl, knowing that you are opening space in your life for new people, projects, and ideas. Experience your new spiritual space and make a commitment to fill it with positive energy. Put a few drops of rosemary on a small stone and keep it with you as a reminder of this promise.

RITUAL REALITY

Every year, I conduct this ritual at the rural conference site of the International Women's Writing Guild. After each participant privately fills pages with her negative "power drains," we reconvene in a sheltered space under a grove of trees next to the main building. There we burn our pages in a large black metal burning pot that looks like a soup cauldron. As the negative emotions burn collectively, the women circle the burning pot, some playing instruments, others chanting or dancing.

One year, a new participant named Dorothy Vascellaro repeatedly spoke to her colleagues about the creative block she was experiencing and its spiritual and financial drain in her life. After participating in this ritual she returned home and found her words; her ability to write fluently returned. She sent me the following impression of her experience with this ritual to share with you:

LAST RITES

The drum hummed.
Hummed as she spoke,
spoke of her deepest fears,
her hatred and her embittered tears.
The drum beat on.
As she set aflame her pain and
her anger and her rage.

The sounds moved her,
sounds of rock upon rock,
beads upon wood, rattling sounds,
vibrating sounds, soft and loud sounds.
All comforting somehow.

Within the chanting she rejoiced.
She is free—free to witness the words
of the depths of her sorrows.
Smudged into black, aflame, then ashes!

And she cries, and then she sighs, and
she even smiles.
She owns her life.
Renewed now.
She is alive.

Empowered by her own releasing,
her own forgiving.
Blessed by the rose scent of renewal—
Touched sweetly by the strength within the
circle of shared lives.

And the spirit of the drum beats on.

Easing into the Unknown

REMEMBER WHEN YOU WERE a child and refused to go on a trip without your favorite toy or teddy bear? How playing with it anywhere brought feelings of safety and comfort, of being in your own room? You had the right idea! Even as grown-ups, we long for a sense of familiarity when we are in a strange place—something that will bridge the gap between the known and the unknown, diminish the edge of anxiety that often accompanies us when we travel, and create a sense of security that frees us to experience our new surroundings.

Whether you are on the road for business, vacationing at a hotel, or living in a college dormitory, it's a good idea to set up your environment as a place to rest and stay in touch with your inner being. Beginning and ending each day in a space that offers peace will allow your senses, intellect, and spirit to explore the strangeness with renewed confidence and strength.

Intention
To bring you comfort and support in an unfamiliar environment.

Timing
Whenever you are away from home.

Ingredients
Cloth napkin, small bowl and candle, feather, shell and rock, personal items that remind you of home, essence of lavender (calming) or floral water scented with your favorite fragrance (joy), penny or piece of copper (good luck).

Recipe
Once unpacked at your destination, cleanse the space by following some of the elements of the New Home blessing (see page 54). Create an altar by clearing an area of your dresser or bedside table and unfolding the napkin on it. Place the

feather, which reflects Spirit, to the east; the rock, symbolizing the body, to the north; the shell, signifying the emotions, to the west; and the candle, representing creativity, to the south. In the center, place the piece of copper as well as a family picture or an object that reminds you of home and security. Light the candle and sprinkle a few drops of lavender or scented floral water on the cloth.

Stand in front of your altar and breathe deeply for a moment. Imagine your anxiety or insecurity crystallizing in your breath and being blown out of yourself and onto the altar as you exhale. Imagine all of your creativity, aspirations, and plans joining in your breath and being held secure by the spirit of the universe. Whisper specific strengths, ideas, and wishes, imagining a productive and happy stay in this place. End the ritual by closing your eyes and taking several cleansing breaths. Extinguish the candle and, except for the essence of lavender, pack away all of the ritual ingredients to use again whenever you choose. Before retiring, place a few drops of the lavender on your pillow.

RITUAL REALITY

Alice, a teacher in Miami, accidentally discovered the power of ritual when she was a Peace Corps volunteer in a rural village in Belize. She had no electricity or running water, and a hole in the floor of her makeshift cabin served as a drain when she bathed with water ladled from the community rain tank. Although she had a strong commitment to her work and her love for the people continued to warm her heart, she felt increasingly homesick.

When the sun went down each evening, Alice closed the wooden shutters for maximum privacy and lit several candles. She boiled a kettle of water on a propane-fueled stove, threw in a few sweet-smelling herbs, and emptied the liquid into the metal tub she used for bathing. Then she scooped up the fragrant warm water and poured it on her body. During her ritual, she listened to the tunes of a British Forces radio station, which squawked out through the speakers of her battery-powered Walkman. Despite the darkness outside, she felt safe, comforted, and "at home," even though she was hundreds of miles away.

Unlocking Blocks

IT'S LIKE HITTING A BRICK wall. You sit down at your computer to write a report, but hours later you're still staring at a blank screen. You stand at your easel to begin the painting you've been picturing in your head for months, and you can't even sketch the familiar scene. Even though writing letters is one of your favorite pastimes, the stack of unanswered correspondence just accumulates.

If you've always taken your creative energy for granted, slamming into this brick wall can be extremely frustrating and confusing. You circle it, trying to make your way over, under, around, and through it, only to find that it continues to loom over your spirit. In fact, your efforts only seem to exacerbate it.

This ritual helps knock down the wall. It will free your mind from the task of performing and instead open it to expression of your innate creativity. Even if, at some future moment, your block returns, you won't need to panic. You can repeat this process whenever you wish.

Intention
To free your creative energy.

Timing
When you feel blocked.

Ingredients
Piece of cardboard and dark-colored marker, cookie tray, water, hammer, orange candle (joy, playfulness), essential oils of neroli, mango, or grapefruit (uplifting), streamers (strips of lightweight paper, about two feet long), large balloon. Optional: paints or any kind of art supplies.

Recipe
You can begin this two-part process by writing your goal on a piece of cardboard; if it's easier, draw or cut out and paste a picture on the cardboard. Put it in a tray of water and place it in your freezer.

When the water has turned to ice, begin the second part of the ritual by lighting the candle and spraying or diffusing the essence you've chosen. After inhaling deeply, exhale slowly as you hold the cold tray, imagining all of your creativity trapped in the block of ice. Take several quick, shallow breaths as you concentrate on the feeling of constriction. Are you holding it in your neck? In your shoulders? Can you feel it in your stomach?

Turn the tray upside down on the floor and tap the bottom until the ice falls out. Cover it with a dishcloth to protect yourself and, with all your might, smash the ice with the hammer. As you crack the physical ice that contains your piece of cardboard, you're breaking the spiritual block that has restricted your creativity. While you clean up, think about all the things you choose to accomplish and sit down and write them on separate streamers. Then, securely attach each streamer to the balloon, take it outside and release it, sending your vision out into the universe.

RITUAL REALITY

Over the years, I've learned to listen very carefully to my clients, knowing that if I do, they will not only tell me the problem but will give me a way to solve it. Diana's story proves my point. A graphic artist, she called me from her home studio in southern Michigan. "I feel all dried up, like I'll never have another creative thought in my head," she wailed. "I really think I'm through. This has been going on for weeks and I have to do *so much work.* . . ."

Ah ha! I remember Diana as a child who absolutely *loved* to paint and draw pictures; she was certain that the best gift she could give was one of her creations. Later, when she was in art school, her creativity bloomed and her finished pieces reflected her joy in her own talent. Somehow over the years, something had clearly happened to her joy; from the sound of her voice and the words she chose, it seemed that her pleasure had been transformed into drudgery. No wonder she was blocked!

I told her about my ritual and suggested that she photocopy the invoices for the overdue orders and then freeze them in water in a cookie tray. While she waited, I told her to go to an art supply store and buy finger paints and paper. When the water was frozen she had to smash it in the backyard, breaking up the *business* of her art into smaller, less overwhelming pieces. Then she had to go into her studio and finger paint, to feel the colors on her hands and set free the flow of her creativity.

She was exuberant when she called me back. She described kneeling on the floor, covered from head to foot with paint, surrounded by shiny paper filled with colors and shapes, singing at the top of her lungs to an old Janis Joplin tape. "I love it all again! Watch your mailbox," she said with a laugh. "You're going to get the messiest roll of paintings you've gotten from me since I was five! And," she added, "it's the best work I've done in years!"

Balancing

MANY CULTURES IN THE world come to a stop between midday and midafternoon. These hours are considered sacrosanct— a time for families to come together to share their thoughts over a meal, and then to rest, renewing themselves before continuing with their work or school. This civilized and refreshing custom is one that we might wish we could adopt.

We're always running to relax, trying to pack our family time, fun, and rejuvenation into the narrow lines of our daily planners. In the process, we run out of hours, arriving late and leaving early, feeling pulled in too many directions by too many people and responsibilities. By the time we stop, we're too exhausted to enjoy the piece and quiet we do have. Besides, here in this rare moment there's also pressure, because if we aren't doing anything, then everybody can claim our attention: "Play with me, Daddy." "Honey, can you fix this shelf?" "Son, can't you just stop by for a minute to help me with my checkbook?"

Although it's tempting, I'm not advocating that we stop for three hours at lunchtime. I am, however, suggesting that it's important for us to discover our own rhythm—one that weaves the threads of our professional and personal lives into a productive and rewarding way of being in the world. This ritual will help you bring inner peace to your worldly activities. And by becoming more aware of how you spend your time and energy, you will nurture and support your own growth.

Intention ∽

To review and revise our relationship with time.

Timing ∽

Whenever you experience time-related stresses.

Ingredients ∽

Two large sheets of paper, marker, white china plate (inexpensive), nontoxic acrylic paints, paintbrushes, daily planner, green candle (balance), piece of amber (helps us discover our own wisdom).

Recipe ∽

Schedule quiet time when absolutely no one will disturb you. This in itself will signal to your family, your colleagues, *and* your psyche that you are about to make some serious changes. Sit down and draw a small circle with a larger one around it. Write "My Life" in the smaller one and then divide the larger one into sections labeled *Work, Family, Play, Exercise, Health,* and *Creative Expression.* The size of each section should realistically reflect the amount of time it consumes in your life. Carefully consider what you see and how it makes you feel. Is this the way you want to spend your time? If you could, how would you change your picture? Draw your answer to this question on the second sheet of paper. Compare both drawings, concentrating on the differences between them. Then think about ways to create a working compromise that incorporates the *have to*s with the *what ifs*. Take your time. The thinking part of this ritual is very important.

When you're ready, set out your paints and create a new pattern for your life on the china plate. Use symbols and color to represent the things you want to do and the way you want to do them. Be a visionary as well as a realist; make the commitment to nurture your spirit as serious as your commitment to maintain your career. Be as generous with yourself as you are with family and friends, because you can't help others unless you first take care of yourself.

Now create an altar: Light a candle to represent your new life, place the amber next to it, and open your daily planner. In it, schedule a minimum of twenty minutes a day that will be your time. Make it clear to those around you—just as you did before doing this ritual—that you do not want to be disturbed during your alone time. Remember that taking time to be with yourself gives your psyche a strong message that you are committed to your own well-being. In addition, it will help you continue to balance the different aspects of your life.

RITUAL REALITY

John had a wake-up call when he suffered a heart attack at age fifty-four. Within twenty-four hours of his admission to the hospital, he stopped focusing on the medical drama that was going on around him. He recognized that the physical aspects of this event would be taken care of by others. What preoccupied him now was the overwhelming realization that he alone needed to deal with the spiritual implications of his illness. The thought "I don't want to die" kept running through his head during his first wakeful night in the ICU. Finally, he felt forced to ask himself why this idea was so persistent. "It's not that I'm afraid of dying," he thought. "So why does it keep echoing in my head? What is my reason for wanting to live so badly?"

It had been a very long time since John had so much quiet time to himself—no phones ringing, no frantic colleagues running into his office with questions, no family crises to be mediated—just John, his machines, and the pleasant but monosyllabic medical staff.

By the time he was allowed to go home, John had answered his own questions. He remembered hearing that when you die, you do not regret the things you have done. Rather, you regret the things you never tried. Without actually using any of the ingredients I've suggested for the balancing ritual, John was able to visualize the whole process in his head. He realized that being afraid—or *too busy*—to live the way he wanted was more threatening than death. He understood that being a good parent meant being a good man. One who, through example, inspires his children to fulfill their potential, enjoy all that life offers, and be generous with themselves and others.

While he was recuperating, John took up painting. The first piece he finished was on a large canvas, full of colors and symbols representing his journey into spiritual health. It hangs in his den where John sees it every day. He always smiles and nods to it, as if the painting were an old and much venerated teacher.

F o l l o w - U p

When you've finished painting the plate, promise to serve yourself at least one snack on it a week. (Make sure you've used nontoxic paint!) Maintain your commitment to your own quiet time. Remember to do this ritual whenever there are major changes in your life or if you find yourself slipping back into the first circle you drew on that large sheet of paper.

Chapter Six
RITUALS FOR RELATIONSHIPS

STEPHEN LEVINE, THE COAUTHOR of *Embracing the Beloved*, suggests that we "use relationships as a means for profound inner growth." I agree. What we do with our friends, families, and partners offers us incredible opportunities to elevate our spiritual and emotional lives. At times, these interactions can confuse, frustrate, and even hurt us, but when we acknowledge their importance and make a commitment to enhance them, we receive their rewards.

Whether you've ever given it thought, you know that you *feel* and *do* different things depending on whom you're with—a sibling, a mentor, or a best pal. It's important to recognize the amazing variety not only among those you love but also in how you express that love. These rituals will steer you toward more fulfilling relationships with those who matter to you by helping you gain insight into your needs and strengths, wishes and expectations.

Bringing in Love

YOU'RE AN ADULT. YOU'VE outgrown the dreamy expectations of adolescence and the painful trials and errors of young adulthood, and now you finally feel ready to fall in love. Then reality strikes. How will you find the right person? Will that person return your feelings? How can you end the long wait and facilitate the process?

The first step involves exploring your own mind and spirit. This will not only give you insight into the qualities you wish for in a partner but also a clearer understanding of who you are and what you want at this time in your life. Your career may come first, and finding a partner who can accept that seems crucial. Or perhaps you're focused on starting a family and you hope for someone who shares that desire.

The second step requires using what you've found out to treat yourself the way you would like others to treat you. Go to movies or concerts you've wanted to attend; have brunch at that new restaurant; buy yourself a beautiful sweater or a good book.

The third step entails learning to really appreciate your own virtues and enjoy your own company. Eventually you will develop an aura that will radiate in the world and draw others to you. Now, you're finally ready for the fourth step—selecting and welcoming the right mate. As Dr. Judith Sills says in her book *A Fine Romance*, "To the degree that you are willing to connect with people, the best place to meet someone is everywhere." You'll find that it's just as easy to meet that perfect person waiting for your luggage at the airport as it is to find him at a dinner party.

Intention

To make a commitment to have a new love.

Timing

When you are ready to be in a relationship.

Ingredients

Pink candle (love), small square of silk—pink (self-love) or red (passion), needle and thread, rose petals (love), rosemary (positive change), cinnamon (happiness), ginger (confidence), rose quartz (to open the heart), love songs.

Start by playing your favorite romantic music. Sit quietly and imagine the qualities that you want in a relationship. What kind of temperament best matches yours? What type of intellectual activity and spiritual focus would be most compatible? What hobbies or sports would you like to share? The more you clarify what you are looking for in a partner, the more powerful this ritual will be for you.

Using your needle and thread, begin to create a simple pouch out of the silk material; let each stitch weave your thoughts and intentions into the fabric. When you've finished, place the following items inside the pouch: the rose quartz to signify your receptive heart; the essences of ginger, rosemary, and cinnamon to assure love and prosperity; and finally, the rose petals to encourage new love. These should be added one at a time, as you invoke a wished-for quality: *This petal is for a loving heart, this for loyalty, this for an emotionally stable partner, this for a financially responsible one.* Light the candle and ask the universe to send you someone with whom you can share a healthy, long-term relationship. Don't try to manipulate the ritual by visualizing a specific person; trust that the spiritual wisdom of the universe will manifest your destiny by presenting you with the best partner.

Afterward, treat yourself to a fabulous dinner at your favorite restaurant, or do something else that will make you feel special. Get ballet tickets or go to a wonderful concert. Dress in your favorite outfit. Anoint yourself with your best perfume. Learn to flirt. Pretend that you are a tourist in a foreign city, and be open to new experiences and meeting new people. Enjoy yourself.

RITUAL REALITY

Five years after her divorce, Kathleen finally felt ready to make a new commitment. She primarily sought two distinct qualities. First, the man would have to be mature and strong enough to view their relationship as an equal partnership. Second, he must be capable of being a good stepparent for her two young children, Tom and Terry. Kathleen hadn't thought beyond these priorities, but she realized that if she wanted to start this new chapter of her life, she needed to begin to focus on it.

One Friday evening, she arranged for her boys to have a sleepover at Grandma's so that she could have some time to do this ritual. After showering and putting her favorite CD's into the carousel, Kathleen gathered her ingredients, lit a pink candle, and began to imagine the man she wanted to bring into her life.

Focusing on what a relationship meant to her at this point in her life was an eyeopener.

The changes in her needs and expectations since her marriage eight years before intrigued her, especially those that occurred during the five years she'd been on her own—managing her own finances, researching the best deal before making a major purchase, becoming more independent emotionally and socially.

Moved by her own growth, she decided to write down everything she'd learned about herself and about what she wanted in a prospective partner. Kathleen rubbed some cinnamon onto the corners of a few sheets of stationery and wrote her most important insight—that she no longer felt she needed a man to take care of her. Then, she wrote for what felt like hours, inhaling the sweetness of the cinnamon and occasionally stopping to feel the cool surface of the rose quartz. When she was finished, she folded the paper and placed it with the rose quartz into her silk pouch.

In the last line she promised herself that she would go someplace once a week so that she could meet new people. Kathleen put the pouch into the drawer of her bedside table, where the cinnamon scent reminded her of her commitment to herself.

Six months later on a plane to California, an airline pilot named Nick sat down next to her. Because she had done this ritual, Kathleen remembered to keep an open heart. Here was a man with the qualities she had wished for. She fought her urge to be defensive and sassy with a new man—her old way of dealing with her fears and the discomfort of forging a new relationship. "I realized if I kept doing what I always did," she later told me, "I'd keep getting what I always got—nothing!" Their relationship flourished, and within a year Kathleen and Nick announced their engagement.

Follow-Up
Sit quietly and hold your silk pouch for a few minutes every day, while envisioning yourself with your hoped-for partner. If you find yourself feeling impatient or sad, empty the pouch and re-create the ritual; this will refocus your spirit and reenergize your quest.

Revitalizing Love

YOU'VE BEEN DATING THE same person for four incredibly happy months when suddenly the romantic glow dims and threatens to fade altogether. His laugh, which delighted you when you first met, seems childish and embarrassing; after the fifth phone call in an hour, he no longer thinks it's great that you have so many friends; and his obsession with the Yankees annoys you as much as your obsession with *The X-Files* annoys him. Communication turns to miscommunication; criticism supplants support; if something doesn't change quickly, the focus on negativity will begin to block out all positive elements in the relationship, signaling the end.

Negative thought forms are very powerful. They can tear down confidence in ourselves, in a significant other, and in an entire relationship. Even thinking about changing those things we wish to change can have an overwhelming effect. Remember when you were a child and Uncle Bob's positive regard seemed to transform you into an angel, while Aunt Jean's negative expectations led you straight to hell? We may be grown up, but we can still be affected by the presumptions of those closest to us.

Obviously our minds can sabotage our relationships. This ritual is designed to shift your focus; instead of engaging in negative self-talk, you can concentrate on the positive qualities that brought you into the relationship in the first place.

Intention ⌒
To revitalize your love relationship.

Timing ⌒
When the loving glow begins to dim.

Ingredients ⌒
Two photocopies of a picture of your partner, box of markers, small notebook, silver candle (wisdom), rose water (compassion), matches.

Recipe ⌒
Create an altar by clearing the surface of your desk or kitchen table and lighting the silver candle. Set out the box of markers and both photocopies. Write your partner's worst behaviors all over the first photocopy; choose a marker color that matches the intensity of your feelings.

Now, select a different-colored marker and add the next-worst traits. Continue changing colors and adding negative behaviors until you can't think of any more. Don't judge what you write. Even if you hear a voice in your head saying "That's ridiculous!" or "You're being really petty," keep at it. These are your true feelings and deserve to be expressed.

When you've finished, sit back and experience the sense of lightness that comes from having unburdened yourself. Then read what you've written, interpreting the meaning of the different colors you've used. Take the photocopy to the sink and release the negative thought forms about your partner by burning the page.

Now sit down, put the markers back in their box, and set the second photocopy squarely in front of you. Begin covering it with positive qualities. Again, choose the marker color to match the importance of each trait. Write freely; don't weigh yourself down with "Yeah, but . . ." or "It never lasts because . . ." Remember, you've burned your negative thought forms.

RITUAL REALITY

Maria, a delicate accountant with strawberry-blond hair, and Tony, a sturdy, handsome electrical contractor, came to me for help when their six-month affair began to falter. Neither had ever been married and both, now in their mid-thirties, really wanted this relationship to last. They sat on my overstuffed couch holding hands as they described the destructive patterns invading their life together.

Maria admitted that she had come to see Tony through a negative lens; everything he did lately seemed to annoy her. She nodded as he described her as a nag, and added that her attitude led him into behaviors that made everything worse. They both acknowledged that they were stuck in this pattern, even though they were still aware of their love for each other.

"I can't seem to stop myself," Maria said. "I'm always so happy to see him at the end of the day, and then the next thing I know I'm harping at him to hang up his jacket, take out the trash, clean up the kitchen—even though he made it messy making my dinner!"

Tony admitted, "I finally just quit trying." He paused and then added softly, "I miss our old ways. I liked nesting with Maria, doing stuff to make her happy. But no more. I never know what might light her fuse." He shifted on the couch and let go of Maria's hand. She drew away from him and folded her arms across her chest. I was seeing firsthand the very dynamics that had brought them to my office!

I suggested that they practice the revitalizing love ritual together. They left, promising they'd do their best. About a month later Tony called. He told me that he and Maria had a rocky time when they first sat down with their photocopies and markers; beginning with negative images had left them both defensive and angry. They'd finally decided to alternate positive and negative aspects. Tony said that this process worked, and that they'd made a commitment to use it, even in daily conversation. He said, "A couple of weeks ago, we both got home late from work. We'd each had a hard day and the tension was pretty strong. I could feel my defenses rising, waiting for Maria to attack." He chuckled, clearly enjoying the story he had to tell. "While we were fixing dinner, I was so nervous that I broke her favorite mixing bowl that I was using to make biscuit dough. I just froze. She was completely quiet while she cleaned up the mess. Then she looked at me. She was crying and smiling and gritting her teeth. She said, 'I really wish you'd been more careful.' And then she sort of straightened her shoulders and said 'Will you please make more biscuits? I love them as much as I loved that bowl.'"

I was puzzled when Tony laughed as he said they both wept. But then he added that over dinner they decided it was time to set a wedding date.

Follow-Up

Keep the positive photocopy and the markers in a convenient place. Add something every day, even if it's simply underlining a word you've already written. After a while, you may want to share this ritual with your partner. As the weeks pass, you will begin to possess stronger, more positive images of each other and yourselves. And your relationship will thrive.

Wedding

WHAT'S HAPPENED TO THE "little woman," standing by her man and serving him dinner the minute he gets home from a hard day at the office? As we move into the twenty-first century, she seems to be disappearing from view, leaving in her wake a lot of confusion about careers versus household responsibilities. Gone are the days when unions were based solely upon the ideals set forth on *The Ozzie and Harriet Show*. Today gender roles overlap, creating both new options and pitfalls.

As a society, we've entered into a great experiment and are awaiting the outcome with our collective fingers crossed. Thus newlyweds find themselves left to their own devices when it comes to setting priorities and rules for a marriage. Economic and professional goals as well as the family's emotional well-being cause increasing concern to both partners.

Not everyone finds traditional wedding ceremonies meaningless, but more and more couples seek new ways to make not only their vows but the whole marriage ritual more relevant to their circumstances and expectations. This ritual doesn't have to replace tradition, but you can incorporate elements of it in any way you choose. By actively participating in the design of your ceremony, by including language and symbols that are meaningful to both partners, you will create a deeper dimension of sacredness.

Intention ⌒

To mark your wedding ceremony with your own personal meanings and priorities.

Timing ⌒

Plan during the months prior to the wedding; perform on the wedding day.

Ingredients ⌒

White candles (purity), flowers—iris, lilac, rose, or jasmine (love), fresh rosemary or rosemary oil (forges strong connection), wedding rings (wholeness and commitment), spring water (purification), cup, large bowl, wine or juice (celebration). Optional: your favorite music.

Recipe ⌒

Create an altar of flowers, candles, spring water, and either sprigs of fresh rosemary or the oil. If your ceremony is taking place in an established church or temple, ask the clergy in charge how much freedom you can have to decorate the existing altar. Select music that conveys special meaning to both of you. Your attendants should include those who have demonstrated their understanding and support, people you would trust with your life. It doesn't matter how many there are—two or twenty—any more than it matters if they all wear matching clothes. The point is to surround yourselves with love.

Ask the person who is officiating to begin with a blessing over wine or fruit juice, both of which are perceived as symbols of joy and abundance. Now recite your vows. These should be drawn directly from your hearts and should clearly reflect both your hopes and the most important elements of your commitment to each other. Words such as *friendship, honesty, patience, joy, goodness,* and *faithfulness* can appear, along with any others that have specific relevance to your relationship. When you have finished, exchange rings with simple expressions of love. (Did you know that the tradition of wearing the band on the fourth finger of your left hand is based upon an ancient belief that a vein runs directly from this finger to your heart?)

Since ancient times, cultures have perceived water as the essence of life and believed that it has the purifying power to restore us to our true spiritual selves. Therefore I suggest ending this ritual with the Hawaiian water ceremony, *ho'o maika'i keia wai,* which means, "bless this water"—taught to me by astrologer Kat Rama. After each partner has drunk from individual cups, the couple pours water into a third cup held by the person officiating. Then the partners carry it outside and empty it onto the earth or into a river or pond, saying "This symbolizes our love flowing into the earth [or water]. May it spread, traveling to everyone on the planet."

RITUAL REALITY

As they plan their wedding, many couples today want to weave their own unique wishes and family traditions into their ceremony so that it reflects their most meaningful elements. Lucy and Michael's wedding is but one example of the many ways you can maintain the best of the old and bring in the spark of the new.

Born and raised in the United States, Lucy decided to weave some of her family's ancient Chinese tradition into her modern wedding ceremony. She spent months asking questions at home and even some time in the library, researching customs and then thinking of ways to integrate them into Western tradition. Michael, her fiancé, was thrilled with her efforts and enthusiastically told his Greek-American family about their plans.

In the Chinese custom, the wedding day began early. Lucy dressed in a colorful, two-piece silk garment called a *kua*. It was embroidered with images of water to represent riches, an elaborate phoenix to symbolize feminine grace, and a powerful dragon that illustrates the bride's wish for strength in her groom. She served a traditional breakfast to Michael's family and her own. It included a tea ceremony, which expressed her respect for all present and symbolized her preparedness for the role of wife.

The families reconvened a few hours later at Lucy's neighborhood church. There, she walked down the aisle on her father's arm to the familiar strains of "Here Comes the Bride." It was a moment Lucy had dreamed of since she was a little girl. She was resplendent in her white gown, complete with flowing veil and train. Six brides-maids and a flower girl, all dressed in lavender, accompanied her to the altar where a Greek-Orthodox ceremony was performed.

At the reception, Lucy—now in a bright red dress with a mandarin collar and side-slits, called a *chipao*—and Michael heard traditional Chinese toasts mingled with the sometimes rau-cous toasts of Michael's fraternity brothers. The couple and their families were moved to laughter and tears, and all agreed that the wedding day was truly a multicultural triumph.

Commitment Ceremony

LIVING WITH SOMEONE—A roommate, a family member, or a lover—requires clear ideas about shared space and a firm resolve to honor implicit as well as explicit boundaries. Citizenship ceremonies mark a decision to live in a new country, marriage ceremonies honor the decision to share one's life, and initiation ceremonies for clubs, fraternities, and sororities bond people together. An old Celtic ritual called "handfasting" marks a commitment between two people and can be done every year. But we who live in fast-paced, modern times have nothing to recognize the commitment made by two people who have decided to live together. The conversations are usually limited to the mechanics of cohabiting—sharing rent and chores.

Everyday life changes over time. Logistical needs, emotional expectations, and even work hours and favorite TV shows can shift without our grasping that such variations require alterations in the way we think and act at home. This ritual is designed to recognize what draws two people together in the first place and to mark the evolution of the relationship. It can signal bringing a relationship to a new level—gay partners, who in all states but one don't have the legal sanction of marriage, often have commitment ceremonies. Or, it can commemorate friends moving in together, lovers setting up house for the first time, or the recommitment of a long-married couple. In any of these situations, this ritual powerfully improves understanding and creates a better home life.

Intention ⌒
To create a beneficial and working relationship between housemates who share an emotional bond.

Timing ⌒
Whenever you wish to enhance your home life, or on an important anniversary.

Ingredients ⌒
Table with altar cloth, bell (to bring in Spirit), bouquet of daffodils (new beginnings) and freesia

(love), bread (nourishment), pine branch (to represent home and security), wine or juice (celebration and abundance), saltwater or sage (purification).

Recipe ⌒

Invite close friends or family members and designate one as the ritual guide. Set all of the ritual ingredients on the table. When everyone has assembled, ask them to gather around the housemates, who stand side by side in front of the table. The guide will create a sacred space by smudging or sprinkling saltwater around the group and circling them while ringing the bell to call in a blessing from Spirit. After a moment of silence, the two people begin to recite their promises to each other and the reasons these vows matter in their everyday lives. They might include "I promise to be your loyal friend," "I will always be truthful with you," or "I will do my best to understand and honor you."

When they've finished, they feed each other a piece of bread, saying "May you never hunger." Then, pouring the wine or juice into a single cup, they share it, saying "May you never thirst." The guide passes the pine branch between them as they offer a wish for shelter and protection. Everyone takes a sip of the wine or juice and blesses the housemates' unity.

RITUAL REALITIES

There are as many kinds of commitments as there are people and circumstances. Many people I have worked with design rituals to acknowledge important commitments according to what best reflects their time of life, their particular situations, and their own emotional needs:

⌀ Paula and Bob, happily married for twenty years, planned a ceremony to renew their wedding vows. They shared with others how a relationship such as theirs offers a space in which two people can grow, nurture each other, and contribute to others. The couple wanted this event to express these firmly held—and practiced—beliefs about marriage in a way that their teenage children could grasp. The invitations asked everyone to bring a photo that reflected memories of their times together. One friend created a beautiful scrapbook with this quote on the cover: "It is the relationship of threads that creates a tapestry." Guests were asked to place their photos inside the scrapbook and write their memories below.

⌀ Jane was excited for her roommate, Kate, and Roger, the man Kate was about to move in with. But she also felt sad about losing Kate's company, panicked about finding a new roommate, and confused about dividing household goods. Jane realized that a ritual would help all of them make the transition go more smoothly, so she asked their closest friends to celebrate Kate's move and honor her commitment to Roger. On the appointed evening, clothes hung on picture hooks and plants covered the surface of the sideboard. Pots, pans, and odd dishes circled the dining room table, which sat like a peaceful island in the sea of objects. On a linen cloth, Jane had placed candles, a graceful bouquet, and all of the ingredients for this ritual. Roger's best friend acted as guide while Jane and Kate spoke about their commitment to each other and how it had evolved. Roger joined them in front of their friends, and together he and Kate spoke of their new commitment to each other. Then, laughing, Jane and Kate divided and boxed up the clothing and housewares they'd bought together over the years. Finally, the three friends spoke the blessings of the wine, bread, and pine branch. Their guests joined with a toast to the past and the future. And they all worked together to put out a lavish potluck dinner that marked their celebration of the occasion.

Clearing Out the Past

HOW MANY TIMES HAVE YOU thought, or even said aloud, "Jack might be my best friend, but he drives me nuts! He's as impatient as my brother," "My roommate makes me crazy—she's as nitpicky as my mother," or "I know Andrew is going to start fooling around on me—just like my ex." We all make these old connections right in the middle of our here-and-now associations with friends, coworkers, or lovers. And when we do, we bring a lot of childhood baggage to adult relationships. Any trace of yesterday's experience evokes knee-jerk reactions that muddy up today's realities.

In order to be truly in the present, you need to make peace with the past. This ritual will allow you to identify areas where you still have negative attachments and free up your energy so that you can enter each situation as new and unique. If you're lucky, you'll actually be able to sit down and do this with those who shaped your responsive patterns or those who can benefit from seeing you release them, such as a partner or child.

Intention
To free yourself from outdated expectations and inappropriate reactions.

Timing
Whenever you sense the past intruding on the present.

Ingredients
Sage or copal (purification), seven-day indigo candle (freedom from fear), rose oil (to open the heart), charcoal and burning pot, photo of the influencing person, tape recorder and blank tape.

Recipe
Carefully arrange your ritual space or altar, setting out all of the ingredients. Burn some sage or copal to clear the air. Prop up the photograph and take as long as you need to reflect on your emotional experience with this person. Consciously remember the virtues and good times along with the bad. Turn on the recorder and begin speaking

about the ways this person has influenced you, for better *and* worse.

Rewind the tape and listen to what you've said. Spend some time thinking about all you can gain from this relationship, record your new thoughts, and rewind the entire tape, which now contains all of your thoughts about the person. Before listening to the lessons you've learned, prepare yourself to release the hard ways you learned them, and simply to feel grateful and glad for the opportunity to grow. When you've mastered seeing the past in this beneficial way, eject the tape and throw it away.

Now light the candle to symbolize your freedom to participate more fully in the present and to practice the lessons you've learned. Ask for support for your efforts. Sprinkle a few drops of rose oil on the candle to bring in love and put the candle in a safe place for it to burn for the next seven days.

RITUAL REALITY

When his son, David, was a youngster, Mark was a great dad. He spent every minute he could with the boy, reading to him, playing, taking him along on errands, and tucking him in every night. Then, the year David turned fourteen, everything changed. Mark had read all about the early teen years, but he was still completely blown away by his son's stubbornness, sloth, and sullenness. And making the situation even worse, Mark kept seeing the ghost of his own adolescence and hearing echoes of his father's voice in his own. He realized he'd do irreparable damage to his relationship with David—just as his father had done with him—if he didn't change this and fast.

Mark reserved a room for the weekend at a rustic inn with great hiking trails and a well-stocked trout pond. He filled a separate backpack with photos of his father and himself as a teenager, a tape recorder, tapes, and a small packet of sage. The first evening, he did this ritual with David. Afterward, instead of throwing out the tapes that he'd made while looking at the photos of himself and his father, Mark gave them to his son. The two made a commitment to each other to sit and listen to the recordings whenever things got tough between them. David was touched by his dad's memories of a difficult adolescence and by his determination to make this time different for David. He promised to support his dad's efforts to release the past and focus on the present. They returned home late Sunday afternoon with a cooler of fresh trout, and without the tension that had characterized their recent relationship.

Releasing an Old Relationship

It has been six months since you broke up with your boyfriend, yet whenever you hear "your" song on the radio your knees turn to jelly and you wonder if you made the right decision. You're in a great new relationship, but one day you run into your ex and all you can do for the next few weeks is obsess about her. Or perhaps you ended an abusive relationship three years ago, and since then have blocked out the pain and can only remember the romance.

If any of these scenarios sound familiar, this ritual will enable you to release the ties that bind you and will free you to move into a new relationship without the old strings still attached.

Intention
To free yourself to start afresh.

Timing
Whenever you feel haunted by a past relationship.

Ingredients
White candle (signifying old relationship), lavender incense (to clear karmic patterns), small bowl of saltwater (for purification), essence of sandalwood (balance), small memento from your old relationship (jewelry, small object, matchbook from a favorite place) or cotton ball, a daffodil (new beginnings), rock (earth), pair of scissors, piece of black yarn.

Recipe
Create an altar by placing the rock to the north (direction of earth), the lavender incense to the east (air), the white candle to the south (fire), and

the bowl of saltwater to the west (water). Place the small memento at the center, and sprinkle it with sandalwood. (If you don't have a small object that reminds you of your relationship, use a cotton ball.)

Begin by lighting the lavender incense. Take a few deep breaths to begin; calm yourself. Light the white candle to represent your old relationship, and as you focus on the candle and continue to breathe deeply, ask yourself, "How am I still connected to my ex? What is it that still affects my emotions? What binds me to him/her?" You may find that it is sexual attraction or guilt; maybe it is unrequited love or the fear that you won't find another significant relationship. Answer these questions openly—let yourself know what is holding you captive. As you name the reasons aloud, tie the black yarn loosely around your wrists or ankles to signify the bonds that still exist.

Now concentrate on each of the elements on your altar as a means of releasing those bonds: the incense of the east to clear your mind; the candle or fire of the south to symbolically burn the restraints on your spirit; the water from the west, sprinkled onto the yarn, to dissolve your physical ties; the rock of the north—the earth element—to heal your body. Cut the yarn and throw it away. Blow out the candle to signify the end of your relation-

ship, and replace the object in the center of your altar with the daffodil as a sign of a new beginning.

RITUAL REALITY

After months of careful consideration, Julie, a thirty-two-year-old nurse, broke off her long-time relationship with Tom. She was confident that she was doing the right thing for both of them and that he would understand her decision. He didn't. He refused to believe that it was in her best interests— or his—to end their affair. Tom kept calling her and every time she heard his voice she felt guilty. Finally, she decided to do a variation of this ritual, one that used the elements near her home at the beach.

Julie gathered driftwood from the shore and built a small bonfire. She breathed the crisp air deeply to free her spirit and rolled in the sand to release her guilt. Taking off the "love bracelet" that Tom had given her for their anniversary, she threw it into the sea. Finally, she took a long swim in the ocean to cleanse her body. Wrapped in a big towel, Julie sat still as she watched the sun go down and felt the strength she had gained from this ritual, certain that it would be heard in her voice the next time she said no to Tom.

Divorce

IT'S SO ANTICLIMACTIC; IT feels so incomplete. After all of the drama, all of the upheaval, all of the physical, emotional, and spiritual chaos, you go to your mailbox one day and there's a one-paragraph letter, written in cold legalese, that says your marriage has ended—your divorce is final. You read it over and over; it's not that you don't understand the words, but their full *meaning* seems to elude you.

In America today, slightly more than 50 percent of all marriages end in divorce and there are no rituals—either healing *or* celebratory—to mark the event. This is true even of religious divorces; while the testimony that precedes a Catholic annulment or a Jewish *get* may be full of pathos, a piece of paper signals the end. This religious document, just like its civil counterpart, leaves the recipient without any sense of closure.

No matter how intense the time was that led up to that moment at the mailbox, you're left standing there saying, "And . . . ?"

I've heard literally hundreds of people—men and women alike—talk with lingering confusion about that moment, years after it happened. I think it's crucial to find a way to experience a healing sense of completion after this life-altering event. We simply can't be free to move forward when we are still looking back over our shoulder.

I have included two divorce rituals in the following pages. The first is designed for both parties; when children are involved, this should include a joint commitment to continue to love and support the children. The second is for you to do on your own if your former spouse is unwilling to take part.

For a Couple

Intention ◠
To bring closure to your marriage.

Timing ◠
Ideally, soon after the divorce agreement is finalized or whenever you each feel ready to release the other, be it weeks, months, or even years later.

Ingredients ◠
Your wedding rings, white candle (representing your relationship), piece of turquoise or lapis (friendship).

Recipe ◠
Prior to meeting, each person should carefully consider what their marriage represented to him or her. This preparation is extremely important; make notes about your thinking, write a letter or a poem, or draw a series of pictures. It may be helpful to agree on some topics. For example: What were the best and the worst times for each of you? What did you learn? What do you now wish for yourselves and each other? Remember that the purpose of this event is peaceable completion; blame has no place here.

Choose to meet somewhere that feels safe for both of you, where you'll be comfortable and undisturbed. Begin by lighting a candle to represent your relationship. Take turns speaking; listen as carefully as you wish to be heard.

When you have finished, put your wedding rings together and bury them in the earth, throw them into a body of water, or smash them with a rock. Acknowledge to each other that your union is dissolved by blowing out the candle. Exchange a piece of turquoise or lapis to represent your future relationship.

RITUAL REALITY

Rodney and Dorothy's ten year marriage ended with anger, tears, and an overwhelming sense of disbelief. High school sweethearts, they had supported each other through college and the throes of starting careers. Finally settled into what they thought of as the rest of their life together, they found that they no longer liked each other very much. Their relationship deteriorated until one evening, after a silent meal, Dorothy admitted to Rodney that she didn't love him anymore. To her surprise, Rodney said he hadn't felt love for her for over a year, but had been too confused and scared to tell her.

Recriminations and hurt filled the period of separating and then negotiating their divorce. They hadn't spoken for months by the time Dorothy found the official letter in her mailbox. She spent the weekend reading and rereading it, trying to absorb its meaning.

Before going to work Monday morning, she called Rodney and asked him to participate in a farewell ceremony. He agreed, acknowledging his own need for a better understanding of all they'd gone through. That evening they talked on the phone, deciding that they would each write their own experience of their relationship in segments of two years, including as much feeling—good and bad—as they could remember.

They set a date and decided to meet in the park, under what had been their favorite tree. Rodney said he'd bring some wine and Dorothy promised to provide the glasses and a candle.

The day dawned gray and cool. By the time they met, the sky was brightening, even though the sun was still hidden. Solemnly, Rodney lit Dorothy's candle as she opened their photo album to the first page. It held carefree, happy pictures taken during their senior year in high school. As the morning progressed, they turned the pages and spoke of their memories, hopes, and disappointments. They laughed about forgotten joys and cried over lost dreams. Finally, together, they blew out the candle and opened the bottle of wine. They toasted the end of their marriage and the beginning of this new phase in their lives. Then they solemnly vowed to remain friends.

On Your Own

Intention ⌒

To achieve a sense of completion and to make a commitment to yourself.

Timing ⌒

As soon as possible after the divorce is final.

Ingredients ⌒

Photograph of your ex-spouse, two candles—white (past) and orange (future), paper and pen, new ring. Optional: wine or juice (celebration).

Recipe ⌒

Before the ceremony, take some quiet time alone to write down everything you'd like to express to your former spouse. This may require more than one sitting but remember, this is only a preparatory step, so don't let it go on too long. Try to balance the good with the bad, recalling your first love for each other as clearly as your later unhappiness. Decide whether or not to invite close friends to this ritual. (I do think it's important to have witnesses, but some people find this too difficult.)

Begin by lighting a candle to represent your married life. Right next to it prop up a picture of your former spouse. Then review the pages you wrote about your marriage. Speak slowly and directly to the photo, allowing each point to fill the space between the likeness and you before going on to the next. Honor your emotions—the sadness, the rage, the pride and the shame, the wishes for reunion or revenge, the exhaustion. Rant and rave. Cry and laugh. Allow healing to begin.

Now carry the candle and the picture to the kitchen sink. Burn the picture in the flame and then extinguish it. Wash the ashes down the drain. Experience the end of the relationship.

RITUAL REALITY

I recently ran into an old college chum, Marcia, and was surprised to hear that after nearly twenty years of marriage, her husband Bruce, a salesman, had left her. He came home from a business trip one evening and simply informed her that he had met someone else. Marcia, a freelance editor, was beyond distraught. Bruce was the love of her life, and she hadn't seen it coming. Worse, because he refused to talk to her, she was left with a pile of feelings and no sense of closure. She wasn't sure she'd ever recover.

I suggested my divorce ritual. Marcia was always first to try something new in the old days, so I wasn't surprised when she immediately said, "I'm game." I warned her that, given her situation, the process was bound to open a floodgate of emotions, but would be healing as well. And, in fact, when Marcia did the first step—recalling her marriage—she spent several days reminiscing and crying.

She asked if I would join her to witness the second part of the ritual, and she invited a few other close women friends as well. The four of us sat in a circle on the floor surrounding Marcia, the white candle, and her framed wedding photo. Marcia played her favorite symphony as soothing background music. After lighting the candle, she tearfully read aloud the good and bad points of her marriage. She then removed her wedding picture from the frame and cut Bruce out of it. She burned his image in a little fireproof dish.

Then we all joined hands and said aloud, "This is the official end of Marcia and Bruce. This is the official beginning of Marcia's new life." Marcia chose not to wear a new ring. "I want to feel completely free," she said. In the days and weeks that followed, she was amazed at how relieved she felt. She realized that after twenty years of marriage, she was so accustomed to worrying about Bruce's needs, that her own desires had often gone unfulfilled. She promised herself that now she'd stay in touch with what *she* needed.

Follow-Up

Within a day or two, write a commitment contract for *yourself*. Include your intention to love and honor your abilities and needs, wishes and dreams, and your feelings. Light a new candle near a mirror; look into your own eyes as you promise to support your own visions and endeavors. Now, place the new ring on your finger to act as a constant reminder of your commitment to yourself.

Chapter Seven

RITUALS OF CONNECTION

Did you ever roll your eyes when Grandpa and his cronies referred to "the good old days," or maybe you just smiled and hummed a little Carly Simon: "These *are* the good old days . . ."? The younger we are, the more we tend to scoff at what we view as an idealized past. As we age, however, nostalgia starts to creep in, and we may find ourselves wishing more and more for the way Grandpa said things used to be.

Most of us grew up experiencing media as the main message, but we've all heard older relatives talk about a time before television, tapes, videos, and computers. It was, they say, a time of stories. Families sat for hours around the dinner table or on the porch with neighbors; women held quilting bees, and men worked side by side, at barn-raisings. They talked to each other all the while, sharing events from the present and memories of the past laced with tales about forebears and dreams for their children.

Today we're often overwhelmed—not only by social change, but by our own far-too-busy schedules. We feel isolated from our community of origin and from the community at large, with neither time nor energy to leisurely enjoy the company of friends and families. The following rituals take our feelings of overload into account while, at the same time, they offer opportunities to renew a sense of togetherness among our families, coworkers, and communities.

Creating Conscious Holidays

MOST OF OUR CELEBRATIONS were created to honor religious or civic events, or to mark the changing of seasons and other happenings in nature. However, because so much of what we celebrate has been turned into a commercial enterprise, we often forget the *real* meaning of holidays. The Fourth of July is now about fireworks, not freedom; Thanksgiving seems more about cooking and eating than counting our blessings; Christmas conjures up images of shopping, not miracles. And as our culture has moved from meaning to material concerns, our memories of these special days are often laden with unrealistic expectations.

Why not be creative? Turn your next holiday celebration into a ritual with your *intention* to give it special meaning; think of its beginning, and its end. This is what I call a *conscious* holiday. Look around you. See what there is to celebrate, ponder its meaning, and think of distinctive ways to establish joyful traditions that are spiritually rewarding. You can even create your own holiday to commemorate a special anniversary, such as the day you passed the medical boards or the day an immigrant relative received her green card.

You can also choose your favorite elements from familiar holidays and insert them into your own specially designed holiday event, adding variations that match your vision. For example, if you find yourself missing your closest friends while eating the annual turkey dinner with dear but distant relatives, there's no reason you can't decide to have your own Thanksgiving supper—in January or July, on a Saturday afternoon or a Tuesday night—whenever the time seems right. Plan ahead. If you think it would be fun to decorate with cardboard turkeys and autumn leaves in April, stock up in November. Put some cranberries in your freezer, press leaves into a book, and make sure your grocer can supply you with other off-season items.

The following is a ritual I do with my family and friends every Thanksgiving, but it can easily be adapted to any holiday. It touches everyone's hearts, even the smallest child, and has brought our family closer together. I hope it will do the same for you.

To give thanks with your friends and family.

Whenever you wish.

Family, friends, traditional and nontraditional foods based on your own family's history, appropriate decorations—for example, spring flowers for Passover, pumpkins for Halloween—two white candles (gratitude), easel. Optional: art supplies, gifts.

Begin by reflecting on the true meaning of *holiday*, which the dictionary defines as "holy day . . . a day of commemoration." Here are the elements of a *conscious* holiday. First, think about the *meaning* of what you're celebrating. Passover signifies liberation; Easter symbolizes renewal; Memorial Day is about remembrance. Second, focus on your *intention*. Consider who will join you for the day, and how as a group you can manifest your collective vision. Next, design invitations that reflect your intention and send them early to make sure that the people you care about most will mark their calendars. Ask your guests not only to RSVP with a favorite holiday recipe or tradition, but also to plan on participating in the preparation.

Start the day early so that everyone can prepare the meal together. Before guests arrive, set up the easel with a clean sheet of paper and a jar of markers close by. As host, you might want to be the first to write your thoughts about this event, or you can leave it blank and write later when everyone else does. Decorate the table with appropriate objects; set up work spaces with specific recipes, ingredients, and utensils. Your guests can choose whom they want to work with, or they can draw names out of a hat. While everyone is working, suggest that each person reminisce about this holiday—their best and worst memories, the best and worst traditions.

When dinner is served and your guests are seated at the table, light the candles and invite people to talk about what has mattered most to them in the past and what they feel most grateful for in the present. Continue this conversation as you pass various dishes and throughout the meal. Encourage everyone to express love and appreciation, nostalgia and hope. Display the generosity of spirit and understanding that drew you and your friends together in the first place. Remind everyone to add their thoughts to the paper on the easel.

RITUAL REALITIES

Holiday rituals are as unique as the families and friends who create them.

🖎 David and Karen, an interfaith couple, decided to create a holiday ritual to bring together the two different styles from their Irish Catholic and Russian Jewish families. Since Karen's family was not comfortable with "sharing feelings," they placed a large poster board on an easel in the living room. They asked each person to write down what they felt thankful for, including writing thanks to specific people. Karen's mother, freed from the need to speak aloud, wrote a beautiful poem to her daughters; John, David's uncle, drew a wonderful cartoon of the whole family; and Samantha, Karen's four-year-old niece, drew her family cat.

All day, people went over to the poster board to read what others had written. This normally conservative and quiet family actually became quite animated. Grandmother Sophia shared stories of holidays in the countryside of Moscow that she remembered from her childhood, which sparked Grandfather Michael's memory of stories outside of Dublin.

🖎 Another couple, Stuart and Cynthia, turned family birthdays into one big holiday. It began about seven years ago when they realized that not one of their grown children had been coming home for their birthdays. After thinking it over, they wrote to each of them saying that even though no one's birthday actually occurred in June, they were designating it as "Birthday Month." The kids had to consult each other and then schedule a few days when they'd all come home at once. As grown up as they were, the children were delighted with the idea—they'd been missing their parents and siblings on their birthdays, as well as the family way of celebrating.

Every year since, Stuart and Cynthia have spent weeks preparing for the birthdays. They build the menu around childhood favorites, wrap gifts, choose decorations, and plan activities. New rituals have been included with the old. For example, each adult child has a special candle that is saved from year to year. During dinner, they light their candles and recount the most important event of the past year and why it mattered; as they blow out their candles, each makes a wish— out loud—for the next year. Cynthia writes them all down in the June Birthday Book. This year they started volume three. Parents and children alike love looking through these books stuffed with photos, party napkins, and other memorabilia; they especially love reviewing past years' important events and wishes.

108

Appreciating Coworkers

For SOME REASON, WE TEND to take positive behaviors for granted. We're too quick to criticize others when they're not doing things our way, and we're far too slow in acknowledging the good things they *are* doing. This is particularly true in the workplace, where we spend more waking hours than we do anyplace else. Relationships with colleagues are crucial—a bad day at the office can mean a worse evening at home.

This ritual can change the way we see others, as well as the events and interactions that surround us every workday. For example, at some point in your life you've probably felt underappreciated by a boss, but has it ever occurred to you that the boss might feel underappreciated by you? Expressing admiration—to supervisors, peers, or assistants—is wholly beneficial. You'll feel better for having spoken; they'll feel better for having heard you. After this ritual, don't be surprised if you begin to sense a significant change in office morale—the mutual good feeling that comes from sharing regard for another can be contagious.

Intention ◠
To express and receive feelings of esteem and trust.

Timing ◠
At least once a month or on special occasions.

Ingredients ◠
Permanent markers, purple candle (spirituality), green candle (healing), sage oil (purification), lemon peel (joy), talking stick, smooth stones.

Recipe ◠
Spend some time envisioning the feelings you hope to evoke in this ritual. For each person you've invited, select a smooth stone and inscribe a positive word on it—like *confidence, joy, patience, love, peace, growth,* or any others that seem appropriate. Find a stick (around three inches thick, two feet long), a baton, a cardboard tube—almost anything can serve as a talking stick. Traditionally, the person who held the talking stick in Native American tribal meetings was the only one in the group

who had the right to speak, to call forth respect from listeners. You might wish to decorate your stick with symbols of your work.

When you've achieved a clear vision, invite your colleagues to join you in a comfortable space; this can be in your home, a sheltered outdoor area, or even a private room in a restaurant. Before everyone arrives, create an altar by placing a basket holding the stones in the center with the candles on either side of it. Set chairs in a circle around the altar. When everyone is seated, ask them to close their eyes and take a few deep breaths. Since this is probably the first time all day that they've been able to sit still—let alone take a deep breath—tell them to enjoy it.

After a few moments, ask your coworkers to place their hands over their hearts and imagine the freedom to both give and receive. Suggest that when they inhale slowly, they receive heart energy from the person on the left, and when they exhale they offer heart energy to the person on the right. Continue breathing in and out until everyone can imagine a band of energy connecting the entire group. Now light the green and purple candles, describing their symbolic meanings as well as their direct significance for this group. Place the essence of sage in a diffuser or burn it on a piece of charcoal. Scatter the lemon peel in a bowl. As you do these things, define the traditional significance of each item. End by introducing the talking stick, giving its history and its immediate purpose, which is to support each speaker's expression of appreciation for those in the circle. Explain that it is equally important to express appreciation for something as simple as bringing someone a cup of tea, or as complicated as listening lovingly to a grieving colleague. Reassure the participants that even if they feel uncomfortable as the recipient of gratitude, they are doing a good thing by allowing another to give in a meaningful way. Giving and receiving is a rewarding cycle. The more you can open up to receiving, the more the universe gives to you. Now pass the talking stick to the person you've chosen to begin. After everyone has spoken at least once, ask them to close their eyes and select a stone from the basket. Encourage them to keep it in the workplace as a reminder of the appreciation they've received and given during this ritual.

RITUAL REALITY

When Joanne was deciding to quit what she thought of as a dead-end job, she received a double promotion. That night when she got home, she told her husband, Bruce, that she didn't know what flabbergasted her more, the promotion or the fact that her boss, Ms. Green, told her about it in the same way she always spoke to her—a simple declaration of fact, without a smile or a single word of praise or encouragement.

Bruce wasn't like Ms. Green. He was clearly delighted with his wife's news; he opened a bottle of champagne and toasted Joanne's abilities and accomplishments while he cooked her favorite dinner. As they ate, he listened attentively to Joanne's vision of her new position, which included supervising six coworkers.

The next morning, Joanne enlisted all six to help arrange the furniture and files in her new office. Wary at first, they warmed to her obvious interest in their opinions on everything from decor to prioritizing projects. They finished at one-thirty, and Joanne suggested that they end the day with a leisurely lunch—her treat. Just as they were leaving, Joanne saw her boss sitting alone in her office; on a whim, she asked her to join them.

As they ordered, it seemed likely that the aloof Ms. Green was going to cast a serious cloud over the party. Joanne knew just how to avert such a disaster. She recalled a friend telling her about an appreciation ritual, and she decided to do a piece of it during the meal. She began by proposing a toast to her boss. Joanne thanked Ms. Green for hiring her in the first place, and for providing so many growth opportunities—including her promotion. Then she invited everyone to say what they appreciated most about their colleagues. When it was Ms. Green's turn, Joanne held her breath.

That evening she told Bruce that, after what seemed like an endless silence, her boss had thanked her for a lovely lunch—and she'd *almost* smiled. Joanne decided that the appreciation ritual would become a regular part of her staff meetings—and that she would invite Ms. Green to attend every one.

Community Building

THESE DAYS, WHETHER WE live in urban, suburban, or rural areas, more often than not we find ourselves in the midst of diverse cultures. Traditions and beliefs differ, family to family, leaving many of us feeling alienated from our neighbors. Sometimes youngsters join gangs because, as one boy said in a *New York Times* interview, "It's about being a part of something. . . ."

As adults, we can provide better options—for our children and ourselves. The first step is understanding that we are connected as a community; the second step is joining together to provide feelings of belonging and support to those in close proximity. To begin, we can pay attention to each other, talk about our strengths and needs, exchange ideas, and create an atmosphere of sharing common goals.

Intention

To establish and maintain a sense of community.

Timing

Whenever a new community is formed or needs to be reminded of its common ties.

Ingredients

Items of cultural or familial importance, special foods, art supplies.

Recipe

Form a group of neighbors who are interested in building a community. Find a room in the basement of a church or temple, or at a community center that you can use as a meeting place. Paint the walls, add a mural, fill the room with plants, and add pictures and objects that celebrate different traditions. The combined cultures will create an atmosphere of commonality and joint interests. Include children in this effort. Give them age-appropriate tasks or encourage them to use the art supplies to make their own masterpieces for display. Take photographs of people as they work, paste them on large sheets of poster board, and put them in a prominent place. Working together, you can make this space belong to everyone.

Have a party when you have completed the renovation. Every family should prepare a dish that reflects its cultural heritage. Those with musical talent can entertain the gathering and explain the tradition behind their performance. Invite your local clergy, shopkeepers, police, and firemen to join you and your neighbors as you enjoy the richness of your diversity.

RITUAL REALITY

Janice was born fifty-five years ago in a small village on the New Jersey shore. During the last decade, she and her friends watched in amazement as their town became *the* place for hordes of ex–city dwellers. A year ago, Janice called a meeting of her old neighbors. After an hour filled with complaints and nostalgia, she interrupted. "Okay. This is exactly why we need to do something. Let's stop wishing we could go back in time and look around us to see what we can do now." By the end of the evening, the small group had made a list of events and projects that would not only include the newcomers but would celebrate the changes and diversity they'd brought with them. Janice's high school buddies Doris and Nina found a large room in their church basement that the pastor said could be used as a community center. Nina's husband, Paul, donated an empty lot behind his Main Street hardware store for a community vegetable garden; he also promised to donate a couple of hoes and some seed packets.

With these things in place, the original group met again to make a calendar of events, which they photocopied and displayed in shop windows all over town. It included several work Saturdays in April and May followed by the community center's grand opening in mid-June. Not satisfied that enough newcomers would participate, Janice, Doris, and Nina devised a phone tree, and devoted several evenings to personally inviting the most recent arrivals to contribute time, food, and whatever items or talents they'd like to share.

On the second Saturday in June, nearly two hundred people watched as children planted corn, tomatoes, carrots, and various herbs in the freshly hoed garden behind Paul's store. Then they all adjourned to the nearby community center to admire the cheerful decorations and colorful furnishings they'd created. A rich array of foods was set out. People took turns singing or playing instruments in front of the microphone the pastor had brought down from his pulpit. Toward the end of the afternoon Janice asked everyone to help her fill in the calendar for the next three months. Her call for volunteers to cover each event was met with more raised hands than she could count. She smiled and said, "Well, I guess we have a real community here." The room filled with cheers.

Follow-Up

Create a community calendar that shows important holidays from every culture. Mark your neighbor's birthdays and anniversaries. Have potluck suppers to welcome new families and ask them to contribute something to the decor. Be sure to add their photos to the poster board display.

Honoring Ancestors

IN MANY CULTURES AROUND the world, venerating those who have died is a time-honored custom. Ancient Africans, Egyptians, Asians, and Native Americans all believed that ancestors lived on in the spirit world and received nourishment from the offerings given to them by the living. Elaborate rituals took place in shrines and temples to sanctify memories and ask for wisdom and guidance. Some of these rites are still practiced in various parts of the world. In Hawaii, for example, every time the hula is danced in ceremony, it is considered a dedication to the ancestors, the elements, and the Creator. Don't check your atlas—just look around you. People light candles for the dead and recite prayers to them in the Catholic church around the corner; Kaddish is intoned in the synagogue across the street.

In *Carnival of the Spirit,* author Luisah Teish says, "A child of God comes to Earth, fulfills a sacred mission, and returns to the Source. But the memory of that human being's deeds serves to guide the rest of humanity." Let us rediscover the richness of our past and seek the treasures of our heritage. As Teish reminds us, "We are the ancestors of the future."

As we learn more about our past, it becomes alive to us. This ritual enables us to remember where we came from so that we can enrich the present.

Intention

To connect with and honor your past.

Timing

Once a year.

Ingredients

Photographs of your ancestors, foods they might have enjoyed, cloth, candles—yellow (joy), orange (health), and white (faith).

Recipe

Begin by researching your family. Look through scrapbooks and albums, ask questions, and see what you can find on the Internet. Write down everything that you think is important. Spend some time imagining your ancestors, their internal and external lives. Envision your wishes for this ritual. Invite members of your immediate and extended families to participate, and when they arrive place a cloth representing your lineage on a table. If your family is a mix of different cultures, lay a cloth for each of them—a piece of Irish linen, silk from Japan, batik from Indonesia, or festive cotton from Africa. Fill the table with foods your ancestors may have eaten. As you light each of the three candles, say a short prayer of remembrance or share a story from your family history. You may choose to dress in period costumes, show old movies if you have them, or play music from the past. End the ritual by asking for your ancestors' blessings on the food you are about to share.

RITUAL REALITY

By the time Linda was ten, her parents, Eric and Susan, second-generation Swedes, realized that she knew nothing of their heritage. They decided that they would do this ritual and involve their daughter in the research and preparations. Susan chose Saint Lucia's Day for their event. It marks a time of celebration for the return of light after a long winter; tradition dictates that every room in the house be filled with brightly shining candles. Linda loved setting tall white tapers and small votive candles on every surface in the living room. She begged both parents to tell stories about the stern-looking relatives in the old photographs that they had framed for the occasion. Her favorite was of a girl, about Linda's age, standing tiny and solemn beside her dollhouse.

At the appointed hour, Susan and Eric lit all of the candles and called Linda into the room. She was so enraptured by the light that she didn't even see the replica of the dollhouse Eric had built as a surprise for her. The small family ate the traditional Saint Lucia meal, taking turns telling Swedish fairy tales. After dessert, they made up a folk dance in memory of their ancestors.

Just before bed, Linda's parents presented her with a beautiful gold locket that had belonged to her great-grandmother. As Linda fell asleep, she promised herself to celebrate Saint Lucia's Day every single year for the rest of her life.

Group Bonding

IF YOU HAVE EVER WORN A team sweater, club shirt, or school ring, you know the feeling that comes from wearing something that connects you to a larger community. Many of us belong to formal and informal associations—discussion or hobby groups, book or investment clubs—but we do not have any outward sign of membership.

Shamans and priests throughout the centuries understood the power of symbol and made sure their ceremonial robes and sacred objects were a large part of any ritual. Even today, judges put on robes, graduates don caps and gowns, and our clergy wear sacred vestments to perform services.

Symbols have deep meaning for the psyche. They are a universal language that allows us to access what Carl Jung called "the collective unconsciousness." A cross, a Star of David, the sun and moon, all speak in symbolic language to the soul.

This ritual, which helps group members create an object representing support and cohesiveness, offers a simple and fun way to connect to your club members or friends.

Intention
To create a symbol of your connection.

Timing
When any kind of group has formed.

Ingredients
Beads or charms (find them in specialty shops or notions departments), wire, bread (nourishment), yellow candle (connection), tulips (foundation).

Recipe
Sit together in a circle. Light the yellow candle, take a few deep breaths, and stop for a moment of silence to mentally set the intention to bond. Place the tulips in the center of the circle along with the loaf of bread.

Each person should bring with him enough beads for each member of the group. For example, if there are six members of the group, each person would show up with six beads. They should pick beads that represent a part of them. For example, one person might choose topaz for new beginnings, another might pick clear quartz for focus, a gold bead for prosperity, or red for passion.

Go around the circle, and as you share what your bead means to you give a bead to another member of the group. When all of the beads have been distributed, use the wire to create a bracelet or necklace. The piece of jewelry can be worn, added to a key ring, used to adorn a talking stick, or placed on your altar.

Finish the ritual by breaking bread with each other, symbolizing your mutual nurturing and support.

RITUAL REALITY

You can do this ritual when a member of your group is leaving. One of my students, a forty-five-year-old designer, accepted a job in Chicago. She had been with our meditation group for five years and felt anxious about the separation. We created a wonderful necklace for her to take on her journey. Each person placed a special blessing in the bead that they gave her, so she would feel like she was taking a part of the group with her to her new home.

She has since shared with various members of the group that whenever she feels low and scared, looking at the necklace, which she hung on her bedroom mirror, gives her hope and courage. Like the teddy bear she used to carry with her as a child, it has given her a feeling of security and connection.

Chapter Eight

RITUALS FOR HEALTH

THE AMAZING POWER OF THE mind–body connection has been recognized in many cultures throughout the ages and, more recently, confirmed by modern medical research. Practitioners and patients alike know that by opening your heart, calming your mind, and directing your thoughts toward positive outcomes, you encourage your body to activate its natural healing mechanism. According to Dr. Christiane Northrup, author of *Women's Bodies, Women's Wisdom*, "The effect of trauma on our physical, mental, and emotional bodies is determined largely by how we interpret the event and give it meaning." Why is it that two people can experience the same event and have radically different outcomes? My friend Jody needs a day in bed after having her tooth filled at the dentist, while her sister Sally treats the same event as if it were a minor nuisance.

Over time, healing rituals have taken on diverse forms. Ancient Egyptians and Greeks poured water over sacred statues and then collected it in small urns to be sipped by the afflicted. In parts of Asia and Africa, people still leave pictures or carvings of diseased parts of their bodies in temples, hoping that prayers of the faithful will cure them. Millions of pilgrims visit Lourdes, Fatima, and other Christian shrines every year, seeking healing in return for their beliefs.

Imagery—using the mind to heal the body—is also common in many cultures, including our own. Picturing well-being can create powerful healing forces—both physical and spiritual—that actually strengthen our immune system, as well as our resolve to heal. The rituals in this chapter combine guided imagery with concrete symbols, to give your subconscious the message that you are committed to your own health and well-being. You will be able to bring sacred healing energy into any situation, whether it be your own living room, your office, or an impersonal hospital room.

Healing the Self

THE MORE OFTEN YOU SEND positive mental messages to your brain, the more your physical body will respond and facilitate your healing. Sometimes healing occurs instantaneously; other times it is a gradual process. In some cases, it is the spirit—not the body—that is healed.

You need to understand how your participation affects your recuperation. Your journey begins when you express all of the emotions that you normally keep bottled up inside. These feelings clog your physical systems, not only causing or exacerbating an illness, but also inhibiting your recovery. Actively unclogging and examining these feelings will lead to instant *and* gradual insights into your methods of coping. If you work with them, you'll find yourself experiencing instant *and* gradual improvement in both your body and spirit.

Sometimes we inherit a tendency toward a certain disease and sometimes our lifestyles threaten our health. In any case, be gentle with yourself. Don't blame yourself or feel guilty about being sick. This ritual will help you to connect with your spiritual self and with the unlimited possibilities of grace. Through this connection it can help you move toward wholeness.

Intention ⌁
To strengthen your potential for physical and emotional self-healing.

Timing ⌁
Whenever you feel sick, sad, stressed out, sapped of energy, or out of sorts.

Ingredients ⌁
Green candle (healing), oil of eucalyptus, juniper, or sandalwood (healing), flower (regeneration), soothing music, healing cloth (a small blanket or any piece of fabric that will be used only for healing rituals).

Recipe ⌁
Set a time for this ritual when no one will disturb you for at least twenty minutes. Begin by placing the flower in a vase and anointing the candle with one of the healing oils. In your own words, offer up a prayer to thank the Creator for the healing that is

about to take place. Turn on the music and lie down on a bed, or on a rug on the floor; place the healing cloth over your chest. Close your eyes and, choosing any technique that quiets your mind, move into a state of deep relaxation (see pages 28–30).

Now imagine that you're surrounded by a group of healers who have come to help release the pain and imbalance in your body. Experience the healers filling your being with a white brilliance that dissolves negativity and brings balance into your cellular structure. As if you were taking a shower in rays of light, see and feel the radiance as it moves into your head and travels down and throughout your body. Breathe slowly and deeply, aware of the light weaving into your immune system, strengthening your organs, cleansing your blood, and bringing healing to every cell in your body.

Ask for information about your "dis-ease." Many of us interpret coming down with the flu as our body's way of telling us to slow down. What is your body trying to tell you now? If you find your mind wandering, focus on the aroma of the oil and the feeling of the cloth on your chest. Breathe deeply, healing with every breath. Experience the healers.

Wherever you feel the most constriction or pain, direct the light to enter that space. Gently dissolve all tension. As you become more and more relaxed, you'll sense your body getting stronger and stronger; you'll experience the light washing through you—cleansing, healing, renewing. With your mind's eye, see yourself as whole and healthy, radiant and full of energy. Enjoy that vision and spend a few moments establishing it securely in your heart and mind. Feel the new inflow of energy coursing through your body.

Finally, give thanks for the healing that has taken place. Name your light-giving team of healers and ask for a symbol that you can carry to evoke their energy whenever you need to connect with them. Know that whenever you need them, they will appear to help you—your own internal support group. Whenever you feel ready, get up very slowly. Blow out the candle. Imagine that the flower has absorbed your pain and disease, and throw it away.

RITUAL REALITIES

I have found that people often adapt this ritual to suit their personalities and particular problems:

 Ever since he was a teenager, Joe, a thirty-seven-year-old computer operator, suffered the excruciating pain of migraine headaches. Whenever the headaches started, they completely debilitated him, leaving him unable to work, play, or even think clearly. By the time he came to me, Joe was desperate and ready to try anything that might save him from the awful, familiar agony.

I suggested a variation of the above ritual. Now when Joe feels the onset of a migraine, he lights a green candle and holds a piece of tourmaline for healing and balance. Then he lies down, closes his eyes, and begins taking slow, deep breaths. He imagines his migraine as a ball of ice. When he evokes his team of healers, he sees them transmitting radiant light into his head, which grows warmer and warmer, slowly melting the painful mass of ice. Joe continues to breath deeply as he watches the ice ball liquefy and drain out of his body. The tension disappears and the headache subsides.

After he performed this ritual a few times, Joe not only became more confident about his ability to heal himself, he also had important insights that seemed to filter through the healing light. He recognized his pattern of suppressing disturbing thoughts and feelings. Now he tries to deal with daily upsets as they occur; then he can release them. He also realized that his sedentary lifestyle and poor eating habits were exhausting his strength and he took responsibility for changing them. The healing power of this ritual, the accompanying insights, and the changes they inspired freed Joe from his migraines and their debilitating consequences.

When Georgia, a high-powered marketing executive in upstate New York, was diagnosed with colon cancer, she was devastated. After reading about the importance of calming the mind when healing the body, she called me. However, she had never so much as taken a yoga class or even meditated. It was quite a leap for this logical, efficient woman to think in terms of developing her spiritual side. To shorten her jump a little, I asked Georgia to tell me her favorite place. "The beach, of course!" she exclaimed. I suggested that she use images from the beach to calm and relax her. Whenever she feels anxious and depleted of energy, she calls upon memories of her favorite times at the beach. In her living room, she sets up a powerful, bright lamp, puts a disc of ocean sounds on her CD player, and spreads a huge beach towel over the carpet. She pours herself a full glass of pineapple juice, changes into her bathing suit, and then covers her body with coconut tanning oil. She lies down and takes a series of deep breaths. Within minutes, Georgia feels completely relaxed, adrift in her wonderful, healing visualization.

Georgia's friends were amazed by the change in her attitude. She credits her healing ritual, which gave her the strength to undergo successful surgery and chemotherapy. Her doctor recently commented that she is healing twice as fast as he expected.

Getting Through Serious Medical Procedures

FROM A DISTANCE, ALL OF us can cheer advances in medical technology that relieve long-term suffering and extend life expectancy. But what happens when we find ourselves or our loved ones desperately needing—and terrified of—the technology used to cure a critical illness?

After a diagnosis and before the process begins, we experience understandable anxiety about the unknown: going into the hospital, the cold, sterile environment, the alien practices and routines, the outcome of treatment, the side effects of medications. During the treatment, our anxiety increases—we lack control over our body and what's being done to it. We're overwhelmed by the medical sights, sounds, smells, and surprises, not to mention the pain. All of this makes it harder for our own natural defenses to kick in.

The good news is that a rash of studies, such as the one conducted by the Department of Medi-

cine at the State University of New York (Buffalo), consistently indicate that people who use imagery and music during surgery lower their heart rate, blood pressure, and stress levels. The same holds true for radiation or chemotherapy treatments—common stress-filled experiences for most people.

The point is, you *can* calm your fears by creating healing rituals that combine familiar, soothing elements. They'll help you regain a sense of control and support your psychological and physical determination to heal. In addition, you'll have a better chance of getting through the procedure and hastening your recovery, diminishing the use of pain medication and decreasing the length of your hospital stay.

Intention

To create a healing stick that will help make any medical treatment or procedure easier and more effective.

Whenever you are about to undergo a serious procedure—such as surgery, radiation, or chemotherapy.

I n g r e d i e n t s ⁓

Your favorite calming music, saltwater (purification), lavender (calming), green candle (universal healing), several small pieces of yarn in different colors, small stick.

R e c i p e ⁓

Set out the ingredients in a comfortable place where you can work peacefully. Begin by lighting the green candle and playing your music. Place a few drops of the lavender oil on a piece of cotton and breathe in its essence. To purify yourself, sprinkle the saltwater on your head and in a circle around your space. Breathe deeply and think about your friends and their most admirable qualities—courage, humor, a loving heart. Consider which strengths would be most valuable to you as you move through this situation.

Select a piece of yarn and imbue it with one of these qualities. For example, imagine that the yellow strand is being filled with your best friend's courage. Cup the yarn in your hands while you remember courageous moments you've observed and imagine each of these events woven into the fibers. Repeat this process, matching various friends' virtues to colors, until you have used seven to eleven pieces of yarn. Tie the pieces of yarn to the stick in any pattern that pleases you.

You have created a healing stick. Hold it in your hands, imagining the coming treatment as a powerful ally; feel grateful for its promised benefits. Bless your friends and their virtues, which now reside in your stick. Drawing on these strengths, tell your body to relax and to work with, not fight against, the treatment. Repeat this visualization as often as you can in the days preceding the medical procedure.

Take your healing stick to the hospital and tell the doctor you need to have it with you at all times. Explain its purpose, or if you are embarrassed, simply say that it's your "good luck charm." I've found that most doctors and nurses support any means to make their patients more positive. Also, see if the staff will play your ritual music during the procedure; even if you are unconscious, it will soothe your spirit.

RITUAL REALITY

Elizabeth, a beautiful thirty-two-year-old advertising executive, was terrified at the thought of her approaching mastectomy and the chemotherapy that would follow. She was having trouble eating and sleeping, and looked pale and drawn. She trembled as she told me that all she could think about were the negative side effects she'd read about—weakness, hair loss, nausea, depression, an overall loss of self esteem. Furthermore, Elizabeth had made a mistake many cancer patients make when they are first diagnosed: she had withdrawn into herself, suffering from feelings of helplessness and terror, alone.

I helped Elizabeth create a healing stick and then taught her simple meditation techniques (see pages 28–30). She worked hard to overcome her fears and her isolation. As she became more comfortable with meditation and absorbed more strength from her healing stick, Elizabeth opened up to the wonderful support offered by her friends and family. She became more confident about her ability to withstand the medical procedures, and about their outcome. Her appetite returned and she began to sleep through the night.

By the time Elizabeth's treatments began, her body's natural healing mechanism was firmly in place, supported by her belief that chemotherapy was her ally. During all of her treatments, Elizabeth listened to her favorite healing music on her Walkman while she meditated. At her last checkup, she was cancer-free. She continues her healing ritual as an integral part of her life.

Healing Another

CULTURES AROUND THE world utilize the power of collective energy for healing rituals. Ruins of healing temples have been excavated in Greece, Turkey, and Egypt. Native American shamans still employ sand painting in elaborate healing practices, using powdered sandstone of different colors to paint sacred patterns that attract healing spirits. The patient sits on the painting while a chanting shaman invites the relevant forces to enter the painting and cure the patient. In the end the sand, which has absorbed all of the negative forces, is thrown away.

Other cultures use different rituals. In Tenganan, a small village in Bali, special *ikat* cloths (*kamben geringsing*) believed to immunize the wearers against illness are woven and used exclusively in ceremonial healing. Members of churches throughout the world participate in prayer circles, dedicated to the healing of a sick parishioner.

In my healing work I act as a channel through which a universal healing energy travels—some believe this to be a divine power, a god or goddess, or simply a collective force of prayer. I do not "heal," but rather I act as a conduit as I acknowlege The Divine within each person.

In this work, I have found four important issues in the healing process. First, if you wish to help someone who is suffering, you need to *ask* their permission—whether or not a person wants to be healed is ultimately his or her decision. Second, if at any time the person expresses discomfort, the session must be stopped immediately. Third, the information that a healer senses about a patient during a healing session may or may not be accurate; therefore, ask about the medical diagnosis and try to understand the precise nature of the illness. You may even want to read up on the disease or consult a physician before you begin to facilitate another's healing. Fourth, do not perform healing ceremonies when you are ill; it won't help the other person—and it will drain the energy you need to heal yourself.

In my experience, healing circles are very powerful and "miracles" can occur. Group healing rituals can give the patient a sense of being cared for and valued. The fact that you would take the time to participate in a healing circle sends a positive message of love to your friend or family member. Further, the more you practice your ability to sense intuitively, the more you allow your own natural abilities to develop and the more powerful your healing will be.

Intention ⟋

To activate and strengthen a person's innate healing mechanism.

Timing ⟋

Whenever a person is suffering from illness or pain.

Ingredients ⟋

Bed or a mat on the floor, cloves (to release unwanted situations), small bowl, tourmaline crystal or turquoise (balance), purple candle (Spirit), green or blue scarf (balance), picture of the patient in good health.

Recipe ⟋

Choose a time when no one will disturb you for at least a half-hour. Create an altar and place all of the ingredients on it. Crush the cloves in a small bowl, light the candle, and place the balance symbol next to the picture of the person receiving the healing. Take a few moments to center yourself (see page 28).

Ask the patient to lie down in a comfortable position on the bed or mat. Assist him or her in setting an intention to be open to the healing process; continue supporting and soothing until you see that the patient is calm and relaxed. The healer, or group of healers, should be positioned to raise hands slightly above the person lying down. (This process will take about twenty minutes, so get as comfortable as possible.)

Begin with a prayer evoking whatever is in the patient's best interests. Concentrate on tuning into a powerful source of health, a universal symbol of healing—some people visualize a strong religious figure such as the Buddha, the Virgin Mary, or a favorite saint. Whatever you choose, make sure that it is familiar to you and aligned with your own beliefs. (Each person in the group can imagine a different healing figure or everyone can connect to the same one.) Breathe deeply and allow the healing energy to move through your whole being and into your hands. Remember, you are not doing the healing. You serve as a conduit through which healing forces are transmitted. Think of yourself as an electrical wire that allows a current to move from the source to the light.

Once you connect to a healing force, imagine that it activates the qualities of the heart center— innate harmony, healing, compassion, and unconditional love. As this energy intensifies, direct it through your hands and into the person who needs it. Some practitioners feel a pulsing sensation in their palms, others experience warmth, coolness, or tingling. Some discover an immediate, natural ability to channel energy; for others it may take months or years of practice. In any case, powerfully holding the *intention* to act as a pure conduit for healing can be enough for this ritual to be successful.

Allow your hands to move above the patient's body, hovering over the areas of greatest need. Concentrate on seeing the person healthy and whole. For most people who are ill, this is a relaxing and pleasant experience. Some even fall asleep. If this happens, simply continue the healing.

When you intuitively feel that you have transmitted sufficient energy—usually after fifteen to twenty minutes—end with a short prayer of thanksgiving. Allow the person to take all the time they need before getting up. Offer him a glass of water and suggest that he take some time to rest before continuing his day. Place the scarf around the patient's neck and give him the crystal to keep with him as a symbol of healing.

RITUAL REALITY

I have led healing circles at least twice a month since 1982. One evening a few years ago, Susan, a twenty-six-year-old actress, asked one of my groups to help her deal with a fibroid tumor that was causing her great pain. After determining the exact nature of her illness and pain, we created a healing circle. At the end, I filled a bottle with water and asked each person to hold it in their hands, visualizing their individual healing force charging the water with wellness. When the bottle was given to Susan, she drank some of the water and took the rest home with her to sip in difficult moments.

Her next checkup showed that the tumor had shrunk 50 percent! Not surprisingly, Susan began to practice self-healing techniques and became a regular participant in our healing circle.

Follow-Up

You may want to have a regular healing circle once a week or month. In severe cases such as cancer or AIDS, people often conduct healing circles every few days.

Dealing with Grief

Y O U ' V E   J U S T   L O S T   Y O U R mother to cancer. Your favorite uncle, age eighty-five, died in his sleep. A college friend is killed in a car accident. Losing a loved one is always painful and difficult—even if the person suffered a long illness or was very old. You may go through all the stages of grief: shock, anger, depression, denial, pain, and finally, acceptance. But you can have rituals to comfort you through this dark, lonely time.

Grieving is a universally recognized process. Hindus have elaborate cremation ceremonies that involve the whole community and allow members of the grief-stricken family to feel the support of their friends. African villagers give themselves over to a series of mourning rituals that often last for weeks. In the Jewish tradition, a burial must take place within twenty-four hours of a death, but a seven-day mourning vigil, known as "sitting *shiva*," allows the bereaved to gather together for comfort. Irish-Catholics hold wakes where they tell stories about the departed; humor often mingles with sadness at these events, when people who have been separated by time and distance come together.

Many grieving rituals include an end of the year ceremony in which the mourner releases the grief and makes a commitment to put aside mourning clothes and return to the community's social scene. In more secular societies, however, people are uncomfortable with long periods of grief; they want things "back to normal" and find it difficult to support those who take "too long" to recover from a loss. But some of us need to take our time to heal.

This ritual can help you deal with the loss of a loved one because it offers a safe outlet, allowing you to express any feelings you need to release. However, it is crucial to understand that you can process your grief in many ways; mourning takes as long as it takes. *You must find your own path to healing.* The following ritual can be a step in the right direction.

Intention

To move through grief toward acceptance of your loss.

Timing

Any point after the death of a loved one.

Ingredients

Video or some photographs of the loved one, plant (continuity), spoon, loved one's favorite perfume or cologne or essence of cypress (comfort).

Recipe

Do this ritual when you can spend as much time as you need without being interrupted. Begin by watching a video or reviewing photos of your loved one, allowing and even encouraging your feelings to surface. Don't censor yourself. Many different emotions may emerge—pain, anger, sadness, even joy. Experiencing a roller coaster of feelings is a healthy part of this process.

To give yourself comfort, inhale the scent that reminds you of the deceased, or use essence of cypress. Speak your feelings aloud, believing that your loved one can hear you. Many cultures around the world believe that the soul remains a dynamic force, able to be contacted even after death. By consciously and literally communicat-ing out loud, you can continue to experience mutual love and support within the relationship. Take as much time as you need.

Sit quietly for several minutes with the plant in your hands, blessing it. Go outside and dig a hole in the soil with the spoon. If you can't go outdoors, fill a large pot with soil. Imagine your love for this person nurturing the earth. Say out loud, "I love you," "I miss you," or any other words that express your caring. Let the plant affirm your remembrance.

RITUAL REALITIES

The ritual I describe in Chapter One which I did to help me deal with my sister's death exemplifies an *individual* grieving ritual. But people can grieve *collectively*, too. Below are examples of each:

One cold, rainy morning, Joanne received the shocking news that Todd, her twenty-three-year-old baby brother, had been killed in the Gulf War. Eighteen months later, she was still grieving his loss, and on what would have been Todd's twenty-fifth birthday, Joanne decided to do this ritual at the family's lakeside home. She and Todd had spent many happy summers there and she felt closest to him under the pine trees that bor-dered the lake.

Joanne packed a large picnic hamper with Todd's favorites—meatloaf sandwiches, dill pickles, corn chips, root beer, and a chocolate cake. On top of the food she placed birthday candles, his high school yearbook, photos of the two of them as little kids, and finally, a picture of him proudly posing in his uniform. On her way out of town, she stopped the car at a nursery to buy a maple sapling to plant beside the lake as a living memorial to her brother.

The sun was shining as she arranged the food and photographs on the picnic table next to the deserted cottage. Her eyes focused on the picture of Todd in his uniform and she gave vent to her rage at his choice to join the armed forces. Then she began to cry, allowing her tears to water the young tree as she planted it. Joanne ended the ritual by lighting the candles on the cake and singing "Happy Birthday" to Todd.

✐ A heartbreaking example of a collective grief ritual took place on September 7, 1997, as millions of people participated in the funeral of Diana, Princess of Wales. This was one of the greatest spontaneous rituals of grief seen during this century. For weeks afterward, people from all classes, religions, and countries left flowers, lit candles, and shared their feelings in public; surprising, some thought, for the normally restrained and private British way of life. *The New York Times* reported that more than a million bouquets of flowers were stacked outside the royal palaces. Over five million people in the United States watched the funeral procession on television. Millions more wore black ribbons; British embassies around the world were inundated with cards and flowers.

Uncharacteristic as it may have been for the English, it was this enormous outpouring of grief that allowed people to begin to heal from the loss. It was a time to honor their princess as well as an outpouring of grief, one that helped family, friends, and strangers begin to heal from an important loss.

F o l l o w - U p

Do this ritual as often as you need to; there is no time limit to grief. Keep the plant in a visible place; you can also transplant it outside.

Chapter Nine

WOMEN'S RITUALS

WOMEN NURTURE. THIS HAS been the expectation, experience, timeless lore, and historic fact of our lives. Not until this century have we started to ask the meaning or the cost of this age-old assumption. Why has nurturing become our exclusive domain? What happens to our own needs when we're so focused on those of others? Who tends to *our* wishes, *our* desires? When do we find time to replenish our inner resources? If we don't recognize and honor our own stored emotions, we not only do ourselves a disservice, our loved ones suffer, too. We have nothing left to give. Where do *we* go for help?

Throughout history, women bonded together as they did traditional "women's work." They received understanding, consolation, support, and even humor from their communal work—cooking, sewing, and child care. Today, however, many women have careers based on male role models and they have become more and more isolated from each other.

The truth is, many of us have lost the wisdom of our grandmothers—their gentleness, their sense of community, and their easy sharing. We must reclaim our heritage as women. There was a time in history when women *and* men honored the female deity. As Merlin Stone shares in *Ancient Mirrors of Womanhood*, "Regardless of race or religion, women from around the world are reclaiming the Goddess within themselves. There is an understanding that she is within all life, and that all life is sacred."

The rituals in this chapter have a twofold purpose: to empower women so that they will recognize and celebrate their true strength and talent, and to support women in accepting, honoring, and meeting their own physical and emotional needs.

Celebrating Your Sensuality

THE ANCIENTS HONORED female sexuality as a regenerative power blessed by the gods. Astarte, the Phoenician goddess of beauty, fertility, and love, was more celebrated than any other deity. She was known as Isis in Egypt, Aphrodite in Greece, Ishtar in Babylonia, Inanna in Sumaria, and Venus in Rome.

But today society has come to fear and even denigrate women's sexuality, and as a result many of us have lost touch with our sexual energy and our natural ability to experience ecstasy. As Andrew Harvey and Anne Baring conclude in *The Divine Feminine*, "Where Aphrodite is not honored, she returns in negative form as the sexual compulsions, pornography, and sadistic fantasies that have taken possession of our culture." We see this time and again in the media—consider the female characters in *Basic Instinct* and *Fatal Attraction*, or in so many popular music videos.

However, women are beginning to reclaim the sexual and sensual goddess within. We are relearning to love our bodies and our innate beauty.

We're recognizing that we don't need to emulate rock singers, models, or movie stars to get in touch with the seductress living inside of us. She is waiting to be released—vibrant, confident, and totally in synch with her sexuality. She loves to touch and be touched. She loves the feeling of silk against her skin, a warm bubble bath, fresh flowers, exotic scents. With practice, we can learn to see her, enjoy her, and own her as a vital part of our own being.

Intention

To awaken the sensuality within.

Timing

Whenever you wish—but particularly when you feel disconnected from your sexual self; before bed is an ideal time, but you can perform this ritual anytime—just give yourself at least an hour and a half to enjoy it.

Ingredients

Red candle (passion), essence of ylang-ylang or

jasmine (sensuality), your favorite perfume, chocolate (sensuality), sensuous music. Optional: silk sheets (sensuality).

Prepare this wonderful tonic to drink at the close of this ritual, which will delight your senses and unleash your nascent sensuality: Blend ½ cup papaya juice, ¼ cup mashed banana, ¼ cup watermelon juice, and ½ teaspoon cloves (optional). Or you might prefer to mix a cup of milk with a dash of cinnamon and a splash of rose water. If none of these are available, set out hot chocolate, grape juice, or a glass of red wine.

Recipe ⌒

Create a sensual atmosphere that will entice your inner seductress to come out of hiding. Find a time when no one will disturb you. Turn off the phones. Put fresh sheets on your bed—silk would be great! Turn down the lights and light the candle. Place a few drops of the essential oil in a diffuser.

Anoint yourself with your favorite perfume, concentrating on the areas between your breasts and near your pubic bone. Lie down on your back with your knees bent and open. Begin to inhale, slowly and deeply, to the count of four; then, exhale in the same manner. Now experience your breathing as if the air were moving through your vagina. Continue until you feel these breaths connecting you to your deepest being. Let the breath flow like a river of energy. Feel the fluidity—the sensuality—and envision a passionate woman inside who wants to talk to you. Imagine that she wants to tell you about herself. Ask her questions: What kinds of clothes does she like? What are her favorite foods? What makes her happy emotionally, physically? What is her relationship with your body? How does she like to be touched? What does she want from you?

Allow this energy—which emanates from your passionate being—to infuse you. Remember this is your own creation, a part of yourself, so don't censor any words or feelings. Be open to learning.

When you're ready, get up slowly. Run a warm bath, adding the oils of your choice. Start your favorite music and set the candle near the tub. Let your body melt into the fragrant water, touching yourself in whatever ways feel best.

Afterward, dry off with a warm towel, get back into bed, and drink your wonderful tonic. Sip it slowly. Let yourself *feel* and *become* that sensual woman. Fantasize, fantasize, fantasize, and immerse yourself in the feeling of hedonistic delight.

RITUAL REALITY

Sandra, a successful thirty-two-year-old businesswoman, had spent the past ten years looking to male mentors for help in advancing her high-powered career. When she began to realize that this effort had eclipsed her sense of self as a woman, she came to me for help. She spoke about her longing to get in touch with her own femininity, to bring romance and passion into her life. She realized that a part of her wished for beautiful lingerie, exquisite scents, and the feeling of being pampered, all of which she had been denying herself.

The ritual we created had two parts. First, I sent Sandra on a treasure hunt to buy silk under-garments and sensual body oils. She was delighted with the process. Instead of taking only a few minutes away from her office, Sandra spent two hours trying on beautiful lacy underwear and nightgowns. She tested oils and perfumes to her heart's content, and chose several different scents. When she got home, she laid out her favorites and prepared to celebrate her sensuality, following the above recipe.

The second part of Sandra's ritual was designed to enhance her progress. It was spread out over time and included an ongoing conversation with her inner passionate self. Her goal was to discover the qualities that she wanted in a rela-tionship, especially how she wanted to feel physically as well as emotionally. She treated her-self to wonderful aromatherapy massages with Suzanne, her favorite masseuse. Every workday, Sandra wore sexy underwear beneath her business suits. She kept fresh flowers in her office. She soon began to notice that men seemed to take more of an interest in her. Most important, the more sen-sual she felt, the more confident she became.

Follow-Up

Spend a few moments every day
appreciating the sensuality
of your body. Keep fragrant oils,
perfumes, and scented candles
in your bedroom and bathroom.

Prenuptial Celebration

WE'VE INHERITED THE IDEA of prenuptial rites from our ancestors all over the world. Early European, African, and Asian societies sanctioned unions involving very young girls who required rigorous instruction in the marital arts. Conducted by the more experienced women of the community, these practical lessons evolved into elaborate rituals. While preparing young women for everything from the duties of a housewife to defloration, these rites carried within them strengthening, spiritual aspects, such as a sense of community among women, renewal for the elders, and reassurance for the bride.

Over time and with changing cultural realities, the centrality of these rites of passage has diminished, together with their spiritual benefits. The prenuptial practices that remain emphasize instead accumulating material things and having a kind of transitory fun. For example, most bridal showers or bachelorette parties catch the imagination only in terms of what gifts to buy, what food to serve, and what games to play.

This ritual will recapture the lost spiritual elements by bringing women together to honor the sacred journey into the state of matrimony, and to remember the significance of the event.

Intention

To create a circle of kinship and support.

Timing

Any time within a few days or months before the wedding.

Ingredients

Music, gardenias (sensuality), incense of ylang-ylang (joy), rose (love), and jasmine (sensuality), picture or statue of butterfly (to symbolize metamorphosis), saltwater (purification), rose water (open heart), cup, egg (wholeness), gold and silver candles (male and female), small bowl, something old (preferably from mother or grandmother), something new (from friends), something borrowed (from the woman with the most children or who comes from the biggest family), something blue (to symbolize The Goddess).

Recipe ⌒

Begin by gathering the bride's closest female friends and family members, and designate one to act as guide. Play some gentle background music and light the incense of your choice to summon joy, love, or sensuality. Make an altar for the butterfly, candles, and flowers. Seat everyone in a circle around the altar and ask them to hold hands, breathing deeply and quietly for a minute or two.

Pass around a bowl of rose water and allow each woman to take a sip. This practice opens hearts and symbolically connects the circle into a sacred container, supporting the bride-to-be on her journey into marriage. Ask the bride to hold an egg with both hands and to share her fears and insecurities, as well as all of the things she doesn't want to bring into her marriage. The egg symbolically absorbs the energy from these concerns, and then the bride breaks it into one of the bowls and throws it away. Give her a small glass of saltwater to cleanse her spirit for her marriage.

Have the future bride share her hopes and dreams, ending with the vows she makes to herself for her married life. These should include a promise to honor and respect her inner self, to nurture her own growth as she will her husband's,

and always to be honest with herself and with him. After voicing support for the bride's vows, the guests give her gifts, which can range from heirlooms to sexy lingerie, from the practical (like recipes or appliances) to the symbolic (tokens of encouragement, humor, and love).

After all of the gifts have been opened, give something old to represent her family line. If the bride's mother or grandmother is there, she should be the one to bridge the connection between the prospective bride's life and her lineage. A friend, or someone representing the groom's family, presents her with something new to represent the new family she is creating. As a symbol of fertility, the woman with the most children, or someone who has many siblings, will loan the bride-to-be something to wear at the wedding ceremony, such as a small piece of jewelry, a ribbon to pin under her skirt, or a hairpin. Then the entire group gives her something blue, such as a garter, to bring Goddess energy into her marriage. Ask each guest to offer a few words of marriage wisdom with her gift.

Finally, have the bride light the two candles—the silver representing herself, the gold representing her future husband. A few moments of silence will follow; the bride expresses her gratitude for the support she has received from her friends and family. Serve the food and drink.

RITUAL REALITY

Donna had recently graduated from college with a degree in communications when she met Tom. Excited both to begin her career in television production and also determined to make a go of this new relationship, she successfully juggled both parts of her life. Two years later, she and Tom announced their engagement. By this time Donna had enormous responsibilities as an assistant producer; planning for a big, fancy wedding stressed her out completely. Her friends, who originally thought about giving her a traditional shower, responded to her anxiety by creating a more soothing and spiritual event.

At the designated time, Donna arrived at her friend Jessica's house, anticipating an evening of bawdy jokes, raucous laughter, and too much rich food. Jessica greeted her calmly at the front door. As they entered the living room, Donna saw what looked like hundreds of candles flickering and softly illuminating a circle of her sisters, closest friends, favorite aunt, and mother, who rang a small bell to signify a beginning.

Donna was amazed by the peace and beauty she felt flowing toward her from her loved ones. She listened in fascination when her aunt explained that the goblet of blended rose water and lemon essence that she passed around would open and purify the hearts of those who sipped from it. Stories followed. The married women told about their experience of marital goodness and hardship, adding lessons they'd learned; the single women envisioned their dreams of marriage. Her sister Jan ended this part of the evening by reading a passage from Kahlil Gibran's *The Prophet*, which begins, "Love one another, but make not a bond of love: Let it rather be a moving sea between the shores of your souls."

With tears in her eyes, Donna thanked everyone. Her sisters rose, lit a candle, and set it beside her—it was her turn now to share her own dreams of marriage as well as her anxieties. After she finished, her mother extinguished the candle and placed it in a teak box—the first of many wonderful gifts she received. Then the women served a ritual meal, full of favorite foods from her childhood through the present. By the end of the evening, Donna felt more dedicated and prepared to enter this new phase of her life.

Finding Your Power

WHAT DOES IT MEAN TO BE a really powerful woman? Although we've seen many changes since the feminist movement of the early seventies, people continue to debate what it means for a woman to identify, use, and enjoy her power. Even today, the idea of women in leadership roles still leads to negative images that reinforce existing stereotypes. We have yet to elect a woman to the presidency—let alone to a majority in the legislature.

Indeed, women are redefining the old model of "power-over," viewing aggression, hierarchy, and confrontation—staples of masculine power—not only as harmful but as counterproductive. At the same time, many women also see the feminine model of "power-under"—going along to get along—as equally harmful and counterproductive. For both genders, true power doesn't rely on game playing, instead it resides in being true to yourself. Sometimes you will lead, sometimes follow, sometimes assert yourself and take a healthy stand for what you want and believe to be right, and sometimes comply and agree for the good of a larger purpose.

As women, we need to take risks with our real, innate strengths. We must use our intuition and rely on our ability to collaborate. This, in fact, represents a new paradigm embraced increasingly by women *and* men. Instead of falling prey to a win/lose mentality, we can seek win/win situations at work, in our relationships, and in our families.

The first step is to appreciate your own unique talents. Identify them. Value them. Take ownership of them. Have the courage to use them well. To help you in this process, I have drawn from a Native American practice: creating symbolic artifacts that acknowledge special gifts and thereby empower people as they move through various rites of passage or embark on a difficult journey or task. The Navajos, for example, made a "medicine shield" for this purpose—a frame made from branches, covered in soft leather or canvas. This shield was viewed as a source of comfort, protection from fear, and reminder of the wearer's connection to the sacred. For centuries, men and women have imbued articles of clothing with symbolic meaning—judges' robes, prayer shawls, policemen's uniforms, or shamanic headdresses.

Instead of a medicine shield, I have adapted this practice to create a symbolic tank top, which I call a "medicine shirt." Whenever you wear it, the qualities it represents will be more accessible to you.

Intention

To release self-imposed limitations and see the powerful woman inside of you.

Timing

When you feel dominated by others and out of touch with your own power.

Ingredients

Gold candle (self-confidence), ginger water (courage), bergamot oil (calming), cotton ball, dill (clarity), white tank top, many colored fabric markers, inspiring music.

Recipe

Find a space where you can easily move around and where no one will disturb you. Set out all of the ingredients, then light the candle. Place a few drops of the bergamot oil on a cotton ball and inhale the aroma, directing any fear or personal deterrents to leave your body. Imagine this negativity moving from the top of your head, through your torso and limbs, and out through the bottoms of your feet.

Now take several deep, slow breaths and meditate on your own unique gifts. Give yourself credit and don't downplay your accomplishments. When you feel secure enough in your inventory of gifts, begin to inhale the dill aroma and concentrate on the qualities you need to develop. Allow an image—an animal or goddess representing those qualities—to come to mind. You might see a lion for leadership, a bear for courage, an ant for patience, an eagle for perspective, a dog for loyalty, or a dolphin for playfulness. Or you might envision the goddess Isis as a symbol of nurturing, Brigit or Sarasvati for confidence, Lilith for perception, Sophia for wisdom, Baubo and Sheela na Gig for laughter, Amaterasu Omikami for boldness, Oshun for joy and sensuality, or Coatlicue for divine direction.

When you have a clear impression, begin to draw or paint on your tank top the symbols and pictures that represent the powers you need. For inspiration, play the music you have chosen. (I prefer Helen Reddy's *I Am Woman; Matriarch*, a CD of Native American women's chants; *Ancient Mother*; or other women's music.) When you're finished, sip the ginger water, and, when the tank top is dry, put it on. Absorb the qualities depicted on your medicine shirt.

RITUAL REALITY

At their monthly meeting, several recently divorced women offered each other understanding and support. They all agreed that they felt safe together, even powerful, but in the outside world they still grew shaky, often overcome by anxiety and a sense of inadequacy. I met with them to develop a ritual that would help them hold on to their feelings of security and confidence, even when they weren't together. After I described the above ritual, they decided that instead of making medicine shirts, they would create power pendants—an article they all felt more comfortable wearing.

The women bought stones in many different colors to represent various qualities they hoped to incorporate into their lives. As they sat together constructing their pendants, each woman dis-

cussed the ways she hoped to use these strengths. They concluded the ritual by ceremonially placing the pendants around each other's necks.

A few months later, the group invited me to come to one of their meetings. Each woman had a story to tell about her power pendant. Several of them noted an improvement in their negotiating skills due to a growing sense of their own strength. Jane, a college professor, wore her pendant under her academic gown when she addressed the faculty at a large university. She not only spoke well but also said that she was able to handle some difficult questions that followed her speech. Stacey, the youngest member of the group, confided that she always wears her pendant on dates to remind herself of her own worth.

Follow-Up

Whenever you need a boost of courage, wear your medicine shirt underneath your clothes—it is a mighty talisman.

Menopause
Honoring the Power of Change

ONE NIGHT YOU'RE SUD- denly shaken from a deep sleep by the pounding of your heart and the hellish heat of your own body. The next day, you're jittery, quick-tempered, and swinging uncontrollably from one mood to another. After looking forward to a quiet dinner with friends, you're about to order appetizers when—without warning—the temperature in the room seems to hit 120 degrees. You suddenly break out in a sweat—your clothes are soaked. Is this menopause?

You remember hearing all the jokes and the embarrassed comments by "older women" fanning themselves. As you try to regain your composure, your mind races as you think, "Is this it? Am I an 'older' woman now? And, if this is a hot *flash*, why has it lasted ten minutes? Why here? Why now? Is everyone laughing at me?"

If we lived in a matriarchal culture, this time would be viewed differently, not only by menopausal women but by the whole community. Our culture would cherish, nurture, and honor us as we left the procreative stage of life for the next, creative stage. Hot flashes would be seen as power surges, or the rising of Kundalini—the vital life force. We would be encouraged to spend significant time in solitude and reflection. Zulu women begin to plan for this time when they are young, looking forward to their future retreat. The ancient Greeks dedicated temples to nurturing the young "crones"—newly menopausal women emerging into full wisdom.

Over forty-three million women in the United States are now at or past menopause; we need to redefine aging and see it as the most powerful stage in a woman's life. In order to reclaim the esteem and sense of celebration that once surrounded and comforted our foremothers in midlife, we have to view our menopausal years not as the loss of productivity, but as a meaningful spiritual passage. This ritual will inspire us to restore our heritage as women of wisdom and beauty and experience this transition as a significant spiritual journey.

To honor the passage to wisdom.

A year and a day after your last period; if you're unsure of the date, guestimate.

Five candles (to represent the five life stages), five individual candle holders, clary sage oil (the feminine), bowl of warm water, six crystals—nickel (youth), bloodstone (courage), silver (fertility, nourishment), obsidian (inner growth), amethyst (spiritual awareness), and lapis lazuli (communication)—fresh flowers (beauty and nature), and music of celebration.

Gather your women friends together where no one will disturb you. After you have set out all of the ingredients, ask everyone to sit in a circle and hold hands. Invite the spirit of The Goddess and all your female ancestors to join you. Place the clary sage in the bowl of warm water and pass it around; each woman should sprinkle some of the water over her head to open herself to the new feminine energy.

The honored woman lights the candles, one at a time, pausing over each to reminisce about the stage that it represents. The first candle and the nickel stand for childhood, a time of growth, finding out who she is and adapting to society. The second represents her maiden years and is placed with the bloodstone. This is a time of finding the courage to express her unique gifts and talents and of her initiation into womanhood. The third, placed next to the silver, signifies her time of marriage and mothering, or of relationship and caretaking. The fourth candle refers to a time of seeking and stands with the obsidian to represent inner growth and inner explorations. The fifth, symbolic of the new stage she is entering, is placed with the amethyst to represent moving into her wisdom and with the lapis lazuli to communicate her wisdom out in the world.

During this ceremony, show sensitivity and caring to the honored woman as she remembers these chapters of her life, with all of their joy and pain, sadness and wonder. Be prepared for some memories to be more difficult than others. For example, if she was unable to bear children, if she had relationships full of turmoil, or if she took care of others to the detriment of her own growth, lighting the third candle can be painful. The fifth candle may inspire fears of aging or of being alone. Help her to see the power and spiritual benefits that await her as a wise woman.

When all of the candles have been lit in a

circle, each beside its designated crystal, celebrate with singing, drumming, or joyful ceremonial music. Shower the honoree with fresh flowers or place a crown of flowers on her head to symbolize her movement into the wisdom stage of her life. Anoint her with her favorite oil. Stand in a circle and affirm your love and support for one another.

RITUAL REALITY

Fifty-two-year-old Carol asked her close women friends to join her as she marked the anniversary of the end of her menses. A busy, successful singer, she'd never had a child and felt the need to mourn this absence before she could step into the next stage of her life.

Carol loved the narrow river that flowed behind her home in Massachusetts and decided to hold the ceremony there. Everyone gathered on the grassy bank and held hands, singing a song to Yemaya, the African Goddess of the Sea, guardian of the universal womb of all creation. Carol shared her feelings of regret that she would never experience the joy of raising a child. Fully dressed, she walked into the river and submerged herself. Then she took off her clothes and let them float away in a symbolic gesture of releasing her old self. Her friends waded with her to the other side of the river. On the shore, they dressed her in a beautiful new multicolored robe, representing the many opportunities waiting for her. They built a bonfire, cooked a delicious meal, and after they ate, Carol sang to her friends and made a commitment to share her gifts with women throughout the world.

With the new energy she had gained from the ritual, Carol found ways to actualize her older, wiser self. She now runs workshops for women as a way of helping them "find their voices," and she volunteers at a center working with children, illustrating her ability to give back to society.

Grieving the Unborn

MILLIONS OF WOMEN throughout the world experience the loss of a child through miscarriage or abortion. Yet sadly, society doesn't offer any place to grieve this psychological and physical trauma. There are no funeral ceremonies or memorial services and the spiritual wounds that follow the loss of a child go untended.

In our country, beliefs held by both pro-choice and anti-abortion groups can influence the ways society does or does not respond. Unfortunately, these polarized views tend to obscure the real issue. Regardless of a woman's leanings, the loss of a child produces great sadness and pain that require comfort and healing. It is not a time for political posturing or medical judgment but instead requires an appropriate mourning process.

Other societies have a clearer position about this loss. For example, the Chinese and Japanese hold elaborate ceremonies every year to honor the unborn. Family members and friends bring flowers and food to cemeteries and say special prayers for all of the children and their families. We should try to emulate this practice with mourning rites of our own. These rituals will help us express the feelings that, if kept imprisoned, may contribute to infertility and mental illness. The following ritual is designed to support such expression in order to begin the healing process.

Intention

To bring acceptance and completion and to help us move on.

Timing

After the loss of an unborn child.

Ingredients

Red marker (to represent sacrifice), paper, white candle (to honor the child), purple candle (to connect with Spirit), seashell (womb), a white flower (purity), cinnamon (happiness), lavender incense or essence (to release guilt, access grief), black shirt (mourning), white shirt (new beginnings), traditional mourning music such as the *Kol Nidre*.

Recipe ~

Create an altar in a peaceful place and arrange the following ingredients on it: the candles, seashell, cinnamon, and flower. Begin burning the lavender incense, or place essence of lavender in a bowl of warm water or in a diffuser. Put on the black shirt as a symbol of mourning. Turn on the music, close your eyes, and allow yourself to move with your feelings of loss, guilt, pain, and anger. Give yourself permission to cry, shout, bang the floor—whatever you need to release your emotions. Stay with the feelings as long as you continue to experience them. Be patient and gentle with yourself.

When you are ready, name the unborn child and light the white candle to honor the child's spirit. Take the marker and paper and write all of the things you wish to say to the child. When you've finished, place the letter on the altar. Take off the black shirt; put on the white one. Light the purple candle to signify the release of pain. Inhale the cinnamon and allow its sweet fragrance to cleanse you of the trauma that you have suffered. Hold the seashell in your hand with the belief that it represents the cosmic mother—the giver of all life. Feel that you are being nurtured both spiritually and physically. If you wish, evoke a positive mother figure such as Mary, the goddess Tyemaya or Isis, or your own

mother or grandmother. Put the letter in a safe place. Be still and peaceful until the candles have completely burned down.

RITUAL REALITY

Every few months, I meet with a group of women of all ages and backgrounds who come together to share their pain and release their grief about the loss of an unborn child. I will relate a few of their stories, because these universal themes help us grasp not only the range of sorrowful experiences in the wake of abortion and miscarriage but also the awful price of isolation and silence. Indeed, pain emerges from each of these stories— pain worsened by the absence, in each woman's past, of understanding and support. As this ritual dramatically illustrates, women can reach out and offer strength to each other—and heal old wounds in the process.

⬦ Sarah, a southern belle now in her eighties, shared her sadness over the miscarriage she had when she was only seventeen. She has carried this burden for over sixty years because when it happened she was not allowed to mention the trauma.

⬦ Gloria, a twenty-year-old dance student, had an abortion two years ago after her boyfriend abandoned her. Desperate and alone, she didn't feel free to express her grief and anger until she entered this group.

🖋 Karen, a recovering drug addict in her thirties, had three abortions and two miscarriages before getting clean. Her emotions were laced with powerful feelings of shame that seriously inhibited her from sharing—even in this group of accepting women. With time, she has recognized that her participation is crucial to her wellness and she has been able to speak more openly.

🖋 Denise, a prominent socialite, shared details about her two late-term miscarriages and her husband's complete inability to comfort either of them.

🖋 Judith, a thirty-nine-year-old businesswoman, still blamed her apparent infertility on an abortion she had eighteen years ago.

At the end of each of these grieving sessions, the participants held each other and expressed admiration for the courage and faith that brought them together. They toasted each other with grape juice and gave thanks for their sisterhood. Practicing this ritual has helped each of them come to terms with their loss, and has given them increased inner strength to deal with their emotions.

Follow-Up

Do this on the anniversary of your loss, or any time you feel the need. You may want to share this ritual with your partner.

Chapter Ten
MEN'S RITUALS

POWER AND LOVE HAVE NO gender. They are essential characteristics to both men and women because we can see nurturing and compassion in mature males and assertiveness in mature females. However, outdated expectations continue to influence how we perceive these attributes in both sexes. Old gender roles now clash with modern realities as never before, leaving both men and women struggling with their identities.

Until recently, men's roles in society were clearly defined. Becoming a man meant taking a wife, starting a family, and becoming a responsible member of the community. Today, however, men often feel alone as they try to sort through society's conflicting messages: "Grab the shiny brass rings of power, money, status, and sex without thinking about others" *and* "Be sensitive, emotional, and nurturing." No wonder men are confused!

In early civilizations, boys were taken from the women and inducted into the ways of the men during ancient rites of initiation. Often they experienced extreme hardship and pain as they learned survival skills and tribal lore. By the time the boys returned home, they had undergone a radical physical and emotional transformation—and were now treated as "men."

Not so long ago, teenage boys were similarly initiated into manhood when they were drafted into the armed services—with many of those same ancient practices and expectations. If we look closely, we can see variations on this theme in the rituals of team sports, college fraternities, and even training programs of large corporations. Sam Keen, author of the best-selling book *Fire in the Belly*, has said publicly what so many men have felt privately: "Our modern rites of passage—war, work, and sex—impoverish and alienate men."

Since the 1970s, a growing number of men have tried to redefine the masculine role in society. Today they participate in groups that encourage shared feelings and increased sensitivity toward others. They work hard to carry these new skills into their offices and homes, to relate to others with compassion, and to redefine the standards and values of parenting. The following rituals come from the time I have spent with some extraordinary men, including my own son and brother, who are on this journey to discover their wholeness.

Connecting with Father

IN EGYPTIAN MYTHOLOGY, Geb, the earth god, was known as the father of the gods and portrayed as the source of paternal authority and abundance. In the Celtic tradition, Daghda was honored as the father/god who provided justice and good fortune. (Many television dads, such as Bill Cosby, are modern versions of both of these deities.) But the Greeks feared their father/god, Zeus, who intimidated by wielding his power and lashing out at his children whenever he was frustrated—not unlike some modern fathers who are unable to express their feelings appropriately.

Several aspects of our society contribute to the continuation of the Zeus model. Fathers today experience enormous economic and emotional pressures that create tension and leave little time for their own emotions, let alone those of their children. Workaholism, family stress, and divorce result in many boys feeling bereft of their fathers. An astonishing statistic reflects this observation: over 50 percent of all boys born after 1985 will never live with their birth fathers.

However, as young adult males remember the pain caused by having an absentee dad, they try to establish a different connection with their own sons. Not surprisingly, many find that this leads to a pressing need to reconcile with their own fathers. Some have found that while the older generation responds awkwardly to verbal expressions of love, when this does happen it creates a new and valuable intimacy.

Do this ritual alone. If it feels appropriate, after you've finished you can share parts of it with your father. If you don't know your father or grew up without much contact with him, visualize the qualities you admire most in other fathers. This ritual is designed to help you with feelings you've kept hidden and change your relationship with your father.

Intention ～

To awaken internalized feelings and reconcile yourself with your father.

Timing ～

When you're exploring what it means to be a man, before becoming a father yourself, or anytime it feels appropriate.

Ingredients ～

Sandalwood incense (to bring you into a state of quiet), paper, pencils, index cards, mementos or photos of your father, special wooden or metal box.

Recipe ～

Light the incense and breathe the aroma deeply for a few moments. Then, without judging or censoring yourself, begin to write on a piece of paper:

My father is _____.

Include as many qualities as you can. Continue with:

What I learned about being a man from my father is _____. (Include lessons about what to do and what *not* to do.)

I am most like my dad when _____.

I am least like my dad when _____.

I missed _____.

Think about what your father might have been like at your age. What were his experiences during this time in his life? What resources and responsibilities did he have or not have? Even if you don't know all of the details, allow yourself to imagine his early years. Write down all of the things that seem most important.

When you finish, review what you've written and talk to your dad as if he were sitting right in front of you. Some men can simply talk out loud; others find it easier to sit facing an empty chair, imagining that their father sits opposite them. With compassion for him and for yourself, honestly express all of your feelings. If you have strong emotions, you may want to walk around, stomp on the ground, hit a punching bag, or just allow the tears to flow. Yes, real men *do* cry; strength can come from vulnerability. Understand that your dad probably learned fathering from his dad, and so on for generations.

Decide what characteristics you want to keep from this inheritance. On the index cards, write all of the qualities that you want to emulate and hope to pass on to your own son; the list may include loyalty, a sense of humor, fairness, and artistic or athletic abilities. Put the cards in your special box and add objects from or pictures of your father—a card he gave you on your tenth birthday, a fishing lure from a long-ago summer vacation, photos of him as a young man. Think of this box as holding your roots. Take a moment to experience the contents becoming part of your spirit. Now close the box and put it away where you can look at it any time you need to connect to the positive father.

RITUAL REALITY

Following his mother's death, Gary, a thirty-five-year-old photographer, was helping his father sort through her things when he came upon a small box filled with photos. Gary realized that they must have had special meaning to his mom—saved separately, not included in the family album, and all of them featuring his dad. He saw his dad as a gawky adolescent, looking shy and self-conscious; as a young man, his face full of tenderness as he held his infant son; and as a husband in a series of photos spanning the years of his marriage. Gary found himself fascinated by the obvious intimacy and sweetness that emanated from each photo—especially by his father's expressions, which were so strange to him.

That night, after his father went to sleep, Gary decided to do this ritual. He brought the box downstairs and spread out the photos on the kitchen table. Then he opened the family album to a page of more familiar scenes. Not having any incense, Gary took some mint and dill (for clarity) from his mother's cupboard and simmered them

with water until the aroma filled the room. He found some paper and a pencil and began to write all of the thoughts, images, and feelings that the photos of his dad evoked. He realized that the man in the current album was very different from the one in his mother's special collection. Gary wrote his most meaningful insights on a separate piece of paper.

The next morning, he and his father talked for hours. For the first time in his life, Gary saw his father use the expressions reflected in his mother's photos and experienced real intimacy with his father. He chose several pictures to take home and reprint in his darkroom. He put them into an album and included his page of insights. Gary promised himself that he would share this album regularly with his own sons.

Follow-Up

Continue to add to the box in the coming weeks, months, years. As you see things in your father or in other male role models that you wish to emulate, you can write down words, cut pictures out of magazines, or find some symbolic token that reminds you of those qualities.

Adventure Challenge

IN PAMPLONA, SPAIN, THE running of the bulls is an annual event in which thousands of Spanish men and boys dash through narrow, crooked streets ahead of a thundering herd of angry bulls. Risking life and limb, the boys embrace the adventure—critically challenging themselves and fate—to prove their manhood. In the United States, Native American youths commonly embark on a "vision quest." Alone in the wilderness, without supplies, they dare the elements as they seek a vision from the gods.

To some extent, in every culture risk-taking is a part of growing up. Whether we choose the activity ourselves or it is mandated by tradition, at some point in our lives we all find ourselves being pushed beyond our comfort zone. The experience can mean different things to different people. Some find the event itself not as bad as the anticipation of it; others find it more difficult than they had imagined.

Many of us hold back because we fear failure or because we do not trust ourselves to handle the responsibilities that come with success. But unless we learn to face and embrace challenge, we will never live life to its fullest. We will always choose what is comfortable and, quite possibly, get bogged down in self-doubt and fear of failure. But when we try our best to meet a challenge, we gain a new sense of self-worth, of our own strength, and of our potential. This ritual will give you the tools you need to expand your view of yourself and your capabilities.

Intention ⌒
To fortify and activate your sense of adventure.

Timing ⌒
When you avoid growing beyond your perceived limits or when you confront an important challenge.

Ingredients ⌒
Orange candle (freedom from limitations), clay, object or picture that symbolizes an immediate

personal risk—such as a photo of a sky diver or snorkeling mask.

Recipe ⌒

Take some time alone when no one will disturb you. Begin by either imagining something you've always wanted to try or concentrating on an upcoming task or event that seems outside of your normal comfort zone. It may be traveling alone to an unfamiliar place, joining a group of friends on a three-week wilderness trek, learning to dance, or becoming computer literate. Try to identify the limits that feel pushed. Are they physical? Intellectual? Emotional?

Light the orange candle and manipulate the lump of clay in your hands. Imagine that you can imbue it with the qualities that you need to overcome your limits. Envision courage, creativity, greater coordination or stamina—whatever you think you need most. Direct these qualities through your fingers and into the clay and begin to form either an abstract shape, a figure, or an object. Work at this as long and as rigorously as you can. Now close your eyes and imagine that this shape or figure represents you. Feel all of these qualities coming to life inside of you. With this new energy and strength, decide what you can do as the first step toward your goal. Get information on courses. Sign up at a gym. Read about other men who have done what you dream about doing. Know that this is the first step on your journey toward adventure.

Once you have completed the above action, the next step requires talking about your accomplishment. Take some time to celebrate with a friend. Acknowledge and applaud yourself for taking this first step. Remember that our psyches can't differentiate between something real and something symbolic. Saying "I did it!" is an important ingredient in this recipe. It's a way of outwardly acknowledging your accomplishment as well as preparing for the next risk. In fact, this gesture of self-recognition lets your psyche know that you're serious about taking chances.

RITUAL REALITY

Sam withstood the pressures of his senior year in college by doing his own version of this ritual. Instead of the clay figure, he bought a map of the United States and taped it to the wall above his desk, circling parts of the country he wanted to explore. He wrote papers, aced exams, and socialized with classmates, all the while imagining himself, scruffy and bearded, the lone stranger in the wilderness. He bought an atlas and highlighted the curvy back roads he would follow from one state to the next. When his mom came to visit, Sam shared his plans with her while trying to ignore the apprehension in her eyes. The week after commencement, she presented her son with a used car, helped him load his gear, and, proud and scared, kissed him good-bye.

The first night out, Sam set up his tent, ate his dinner, savored the starry night sky, climbed into his sleeping bag, and was instantly overcome by terror. Sam was a city boy; even when he was alone he had always been surrounded by other people. Now he heard every sound magnified and his imagination took over. Was he hearing a grizzly bear or a crazed escaped convict? Had he stowed away his supplies safely? What would he do if an intruder—man or beast—barged into his tent? His dream of being on his own turned into a nightmare. After three hours of sleeplessness, Sam realized that he had a choice: either turn around and go home or figure out a way to continue his adventure without fear.

He remembered the ritual he had done with the map of the United States. He lit his lantern, rekindled the campfire, gathered a bowl of stones, and began to imagine that each stone represented a man who had successfully survived the wilderness. He saw that he had already taken the hardest step (leaving home on his own) and that he could move beyond this next challenge.

He remembered hearing that courage is not a lack of fear, but being able to move forward in spite of that fear. Finally, as the sun rose, Sam was able to go to sleep. After he woke up, he put one of the stones in his pocket to remind himself that he had the capacity to move forward.

Back on the road by noon, he stopped to call his mom to tell her about his experience the night before. She expressed her pride in his resourcefulness and her confidence in his ability not only to survive but also to enjoy the rest of his adventure. Sam drove to the deserts of the Southwest. He relished his growing capabilities. Although he often felt lonely, he gained new insights about himself. Two months later when he returned home, he had a new sense of confidence about successfully shaping his life and living his vision for the future.

Follow-Up

Keep your clay figure visible—on your altar, desk, or bedside table—to remind yourself of your new capabilities. Write down all that you've learned about yourself and share these insights with a close friend.

A Sharing Ritual

IN MEDITERRANEAN COUN-
tries, men kiss each other hello and good-bye.
Indonesian men walk down the street hand in
hand. But the men I know tell me that they don't
feel comfortable expressing feelings—physically
or emotionally—with their pals. They find it easier to communicate with women, especially when
it comes to things that really matter. The sad fact
is that men don't know how to behave with other
men. Our society's macho expectations and homo-
phobic taboos have created powerful artificial
barriers that keep most men at an emotional
arm's length from each other. They use business
meetings, ball games, and outdoor adventures—
even the battlefield—as the only acceptable arenas
for being together. But the emotions expressed in
these places are safe and often obscure substitu-
tions for more intimate feelings.

Yet most men confide in women friends
that they wish it could be different—that they
could find a way to have male confidants. They
imagine that such closeness would not only enrich
their lives and enhance their self-understanding,
but that it would also be fun. This ritual is
designed to help men in their interactions with
each other—to both strengthen and illuminate
their male relationships.

Intention ⌒
To establish and strengthen meaningful male
friendships.

Timing ⌒
On a regular basis, as often as possible.

Ingredients ⌒
Two indigo candles (to trust your own feelings—
and each other), essential oil of melissa (acceptance), paper and pencil, calendar, telephone book.

Recipe ⌒
Invite a good friend to your home for lunch or
dinner. Before he arrives, prepare the dining table
as an altar by lighting both of the candles and
putting the melissa into a small bowl of warm
water. When the two of you sit down to eat,
explain the purpose of this ritual and begin to
share some less complicated parts of your histo-

ries. Start with something easy—memories of a grade-school girlfriend, your first team sport triumph (or disaster), early family relationships—and gradually move on to more meaningful events. The give and take may feel awkward at first, but as you uncover common experiences, the discomfort will give way to comfort.

When you feel that you're breaking through the habit of withholding, talk about building this relationship. Express it as a team effort that involves commitment, practice, and working out with your new skills. Suggest combining the next few meetings with trying new restaurants. Use the phone book to make a list of those that sound most promising, and decide on convenient times to meet over the next few months. Be flexible—breakfast conversations can be as rewarding as dinner conversations.

Blow out both candles and give one of them to your friend as a reminder to trust the process that you've begun.

RITUAL REALITY

Since their graduation fifteen years ago, Jason, a musician from Philadelphia, and his college roommate, Alex, a lawyer from Florida, have gone on an August camping trip—a very tradi-tional male-bonding ritual. This context was the only time and place the two men felt comfortable sharing their feelings; they never sought each other out during the time in between. Rather, they turned—as most men do—to the women in their lives for solace.

One year, however, everything seemed to fall apart in Alex's life. His marriage broke up, his children expressed anger and hostility toward him, his firm floundered, and to make matters worse, his blood pressure and cholesterol soared. In late October, he called Jason and invited himself to Philadelphia for the weekend.

Jason picked him up at the airport and the two men fell right into the old, familiar pattern. After checking in at Alex's hotel, they went to the bar for a drink. Awkwardly, Alex reported the events of the past few months, but he clearly found it too difficult to describe his confusion and pain. Jason watched his old friend's discomfort, and finally told him about doing this sharing ritual with a guy from his orchestra, and how rewarding the process had been. He asked Alex to extend his stay so that they could try it together.

The next evening at Jason's house, he explained the significance of the ritual ingredients as he and Alex prepared the meal and set the table as an altar. They lit the candles and placed the melissa in a bowl of warm water between the indigo tapers. As they ate dinner, they discussed the limits of their friendship.

Then, as if to prove the point, Jason began to confide the trauma he'd suffered two years earlier when his father died. He wept as he told Alex about all of the conversations he wished he'd had with his dad. "That's why finding the ritual was so important to me," he said. "It taught me how to talk about things that really matter, with the people that really matter." With the promise of deepening their relationship during the next week, the two friends embraced for the first time and parted for the night. They vowed to maintain this new level of friendship—and to meet over meals as often as for "macho" events. At home in Florida, Alex found two new indigo candles that Jason had slipped into his suitcase.

The attached card said, "These are for you to light when I call you next week, to remind you to keep talking."

Follow-Up

Create and maintain a small altar with the indigo candle and essential oil. Before each meeting, sit quietly in the soft light of the candle and inhale the melissa. Think about the ways you need to push yourself through to new levels of trust and intimacy. Congratulate yourself on the courage and perseverance you've exhibited so far.

Prenuptial Celebration

In MANY TRADITIONS, THE groom spends time before his wedding fasting and praying. He performs sacred rituals to prepare his mind and body for the new union he will soon enter into. However, in our modern culture the usual male premarital rite is the bachelor party, a last-chance-to-sow-your-wild-oats debauch, during which men spend an evening watching strippers and getting drunk. Many of my clients have shared their otherwise unspoken disgust and disappointment with this tradition, as well as their wish for a more appropriate, meaningful event. These men don't want to mirror their fiancées' experience; they want something that reflects their masculine hopes and fears and their own way of offering support and understanding to their friends. I've listened to them and thought about what I've heard. The following ritual is my response. It is designed to change the way men celebrate their transition from single to married life, focusing not on what they will lose, but on all they have to gain.

Intention

To honor and celebrate the prenuptial experience while bonding with other men—both family and friends.

Timing

Within a few days or weeks of the wedding.

Ingredients

Sheltered outdoor space, wood, paper, and matches for a bonfire, essence of basil (clarity), orange (joy), and ginger (confidence), rose water (opens the heart), champagne or juice (celebration).

Recipe

Gather as many male members of the groom's family as possible—his father, grandfathers, uncles, and cousins of all ages. If he has a son from a previous marriage, include him in a position of honor. Bring everyone together and gather wood for a bonfire. Make sure you have lots of food that you can cook later over the fire.

Appoint a guide—ideally the eldest of the group—and then sit silently in a circle around the mound for a minute or two. Ask the guide to light the fire. Some of the men may be nervous about participating in male rituals, so start off by explaining that the purpose of the ritual is to share stories about family and friends. Then pass the various oils and, as each person anoints himself, discuss what they represent. Finish with another moment of silence, followed by an invitation to tell stories about loving relationships, their joys and difficulties.

Perhaps the oldest male in the group can begin by talking about his own marriage and what it means to him today. Such sharing will join the men in laughter and thoughtfulness, as well as create a memory bank full of wisdom and support for the groom to draw upon.

End the ritual by mixing rose water with champagne (symbolizing celebration with an open heart) and offering a toast—if this is too much of a stretch for the men involved, just use the champagne. Then have the groom throw a small bundle of branches, representing his fears, into the fire.

RITUAL REALITY

Warren's father and brothers knew that he loved camping, so they asked five of his friends to join them on an overnight expedition to celebrate his impending marriage. They chose a secluded place not too far from the city or too difficult to find. When they'd all pitched their tents and unpacked their gear, they gathered wood for a fire and grilled a hearty meal. In the darkening evening, they stoked the fire and, with the best man's guidance, began talking about the changing roles and expectations they all faced. They spoke openly and intimately about their experiences. Then they asked Warren to throw a small bundle of branches representing his fears into the fire. The men cheered as they watched it burn. They opened the champagne and toasted Warren's choice of bride, themselves, and the future. When they packed up the next morning, each member of the group was a happy camper, grateful for the experience of the night before.

Appreciating the Feminine

WHEN YOU HEAR THE WORDS *beauty, tenderness, caring,* and *sensitivity,* do you immediately think feminine? If you do, you have fallen into one of the stereotypes that plague our society and limit our understanding of what it is to be human. Vision, appreciation for beauty, and the ability to nurture keep *both* genders from feeling that their lives are isolated and mundane. Together, Italian couples cry openly when hearing a magnificent aria, while educated Asians—women and men—are expected to be connoisseurs of beauty. The task for all men is to integrate these qualities without feeling that their ability to focus, structure, and assert themselves is being threatened. Martin Luther King, Mahatma Gandhi, and Winston Churchill all represent forceful leaders who fought for their beliefs while nurturing their communities.

American men must begin to honor qualities we've labled *feminine,* just as women must honor qualities we've named *masculine.* An imbalance occurs when one sex or the other connects to a single side; polarities lead to adversarial roles, which only widen the gender gap. This ritual will help men integrate both their masculine and feminine qualities to balance their relationships for a deeper and more fulfilling life.

Intention

To learn to honor and embrace the feminine.

Timing

When you don't know what you're feeling because you're thinking too much.

Ingredients

Pink candle (compassion, gentleness, love), rose water or grape juice (to open the heart), piece of art or poetry, bowl of water (the unconscious and the sensate body).

Recipe

If possible, do this ritual outside in a quiet spot where you can be alone. If circumstances require you to remain indoors, turn off the phone and fax machine. Light the candle, and ask to connect with the part of you that's open to giving and receiving love, nourishing, and appreciating beauty. Slowly sip the rose water or grape juice and imagine that this elixir opens your heart, increasing your capacity to stay centered in the midst of chaos, as well as channel healing, compassion, and unconditional love for yourself and others.

Hold the bowl of water in your hands. Focus on the "flow" of your life. As you connect to the element of water, imagine that you evoke the dreamer or visionary inside of you—the part that relates to the world, that is compassionate and empathic. This part of you is expansive, able to embrace feelings and be passionate about life. The part of you that sets goals, structures time, and defines results has its merits, but without this other aspect—the feminine—you remain rigid and cut off from life.

Concentrate on suspending the urge to force things to happen in your life; let go of the typically male struggle to maintain control. There are times to overcome obstacles and times when it's better to pause and simply reflect, opening up space for easier solutions to enter. With this understanding, think about your belief system. Do you remain rigid in certain areas and refuse to let new thoughts in, fighting new ideas and approaches?

Let any willfulness or inflexibility slowly seep into the bowl. When you feel this process is complete, empty the water onto the ground.

Take out the artwork or read the poetry aloud. Consciously allow yourself to feel your emotions. Where do these feelings come from? How do you internalize the words of the poem or the lines of the artwork? What images or memories do they activate? If you are outside, let nature guide you into the beauty that surrounds you. Absorb the exquisite pallet of color, texture, and design. Notice how the different colors affect you: Is green calming? Does red evoke feelings of passion? Does the blue sky make you feel expansive? You may begin to remember scenes from your past or connect to dreams and visions for your future. Allow yourself to remember the dreams you had as a young boy before the socialization process squelched your sensitive self. Simply allow the process to continue. When you're ready, gaze into the candlelight, and make a commitment to honor the feminine aspects in your life.

RITUAL REALITY

Mike, a thirty-seven-year-old insurance executive, left his office early after a difficult meeting with his staff. Worn out by his leadership role, he felt like a caricature—the testosterone-driven boss. So Mike headed into the foothills outside the city, consciously trying to still his inner he-man by focusing on the beauty of nature. He stopped his car on a rutted dirt road when he saw a magnificent buck repeatedly ramming his head into a heavy chain fence. As he watched, he noticed that only thirty yards away there was a large hole in the links. So intent on forcing his way through, the buck didn't even notice that there was an easier solution to his problem. Stunned by this metaphor for his own life, Mike decided that it was time to do something about it.

He drove away from the struggling buck and stopped the car next to a grove of aspens. Sitting under the trees, Mike spent five minutes doing a heart meditation (see page 28). When he opened his eyes, he spotted a cluster of wildflowers nearby. He selected a few to take home as a reminder of the buck's unnecessary aggression as well as nature's peaceful, nurturing beauty. That evening, instead of going through the papers in his briefcase, Mike listened to some classical music to complete the ritual.

The next day, Mike set up a small altar in his office with the wildflowers and a rose quartz crystal (to open the heart) he had received as a gift from a close woman friend. He promised himself to spend twenty undisturbed minutes every day in front of this altar, just *being*, instead of always *doing*.

In time, Mike discovered that he was able to communicate in a deeper way with his friends and colleagues. Instead of having a black and white attitude about issues, he now felt more tolerant of differences and delighted in the new opportunities that became available to him. He even decided to subscribe to the local philharmonic orchestra in his town, a step his macho self would never have taken.

Follow-Up

Take a few minutes each day to quiet yourself and open to the qualities of the heart center—compassion, openness, nurturing, healing, empathy, unconditional love.

ACKNOWLEDGMENTS

I give thanks to Spirit for always guiding and protecting me, and to The Goddess Kuan Yin for teaching me about compassion.

To my mother, Diana, for her unconditional love and support even if she didn't understand what I was doing.

To my son, Jourdan, for his encouragement and love. In his own rite of passage he vacated his room so I could create a sacred space to write this book.

To my brother, Mark, for always being there, and for showing me what a loving supportive male presence could be like.

To Melinda Blau, my writing diva, who encouraged me from the beginning and stood next to me step-by-step, helping me shape this book into its present form.

To Nancy Walsh, my left and right arm. Without her support this book would have been impossible.

To Eleanor Johnson, the most spiritual woman I have ever met, who said to me one day, "Why not do a ritual once a month in my loft?" And then allowed me access to her sacred space so that I could have a home for my work.

To Pamela Serure, snake woman, who kept me from burnout by reminding me to eat right and find quiet time for myself.

To Pam Jones, my legal wonder woman, for her friendship and razor-sharp negotiating skills.

To Joanne Roberts for holding up the mirror of what is possible.

To Laura Norman, who always kept me positive, and to her constant gift of reflexology to keep my body in balance.

To Laura Yorke at Golden Books—she is a remarkable editor and made working on my first book a wonderful experience.

To Lara Asher at Golden Books for her continuous good humor and keen observations.

To my agent, Eileen Cope, for all her great ideas and expertise.

To all the healers who kept my body strong and balanced, especially Dr. Stephen Oswald, Claudia Ascione, Marie Raiche, and Kavi.

To Coralie Romanyshyn and Mar-yannu Hathori for teaching me to dance.

To all my friends who put up with my hectic schedule, especially Sally Germaine, Allan Beinhorn, and Franco Miele.

To Rosemary Serluca and Laura Marini for their gifts of always having the right words.

To Hannelore Hahn and all the women at the International Women's Writing Guild who shared their stories with me and allowed me to share my dream with them.

To my meditation group: the wonderful women and men who come together to create sacred space and make everything possible. They have held the container that has allowed me to thrive.

To Stacey Shane, my "daughter," who helped inspire and organize me.

To Elaine Criscione and John Ottovano for making me look good.

To Michael Owen Schwager for his dedication to Spirit and the Enrichment Channel and for his generous advice and help.

To John Steele, for teaching me about aromatherapy and for the gift of our long friendship.

To Alex Stark, a master of feng shui, who changed the energy of my home into a sacred space that is able to contain my deepest dreams.

To Susan Rosen, for teaching me about the feminine face of God.

To Susan Peterson and Claire Ferraro for their friendship, humor, insights, and unconditional support.

To Barbara Gess, who saw the possibilities of this book way before I did.

To Joan Horton, Robin Quivers, Rande Brown, Virginia Roberts, Meredith Young Sowers, Joanna Hadjiani, Allie Roth, Geneen Whitwar, Marta Houske, Alicia Schmoller, Julia Riva, Norma and Loren Kroll, Elyse and Jay Grayson, Sharon Whitely, Leslie Corn, Phyllis and Lewis Cohen, Miriam Dyak, Monty Farber, Hal and Sidra Stone, Amy Zerner, Carol Martin, Kenny and Mara Wurtenberger, Tony Crawford, Denise O'Connor, and Karen LeRaux for their friendship and encouragements.

To The Goddesses, especially Laurie Sue Brockway, for their encouragement and practical advice.

To all my teachers.

To Brugh Joy for showing me what ritual could be.

To Carolyn Conger for helping me blossom.

Many men shared their expertise with me; a special thanks to Richard Berger, Dr. Ron Taffel, Dr. Jeffrey Fishman, Michael Goldstein, Dumisani Kumalo, Keith Weinstein, Richard Whitely, Richard Rosen, and Nick Barone.

To Donna Hoffman, Elizabeth Rose Campbell, Katrama, and Shelly Ackerman for their brilliant counsel.

To Anna and Igor Sergiyeniko and Anna Shutaya for their endless tales of Russia.

To all the incredible people who have participated in ritual circles with me. Much of what is contained in this book emerged through my interaction with these individuals and groups. I thank each and every one of you.

SUGGESTED MUSIC

Anugama. *Healing.* (healing, meditation)

————. *Shamanic Dreams.* (release)

Asher, James. *Feet in the Soil.* (celebration, dance)

Colorado Creative Music. *Regeneration (acoustotherapy).* (meditation, relaxation)

————. *Relaxation (acoustotherapy).* (meditation, relaxation)

Demby, Constance. *Aeterna.* (meditation)

————. *Sacred Space Music.* (healing, meditation)

Coxon, Robert Haig. *The Inner Voyage.* (meditation, healing)

————. *The Silent Path.* (meditation, relaxation)

Gass, Robert. *Ancient Mother.* (women's rituals)

Goodall, Medwyn. *Medicine Woman.* (release, women's rituals)

Horn, Paul. *Inside the Great Pyramid.* (invoking spirit)

Kobialka, Daniel. *Timeless Motion.* (meditation, relaxation)

Lim, Jack. *Inner Peace.* (meditation, relaxation)

Noha, Yeha. *Sacred Spirits.* (invoking spirit)

Olatunji, Babatunde. *Drums of Passion.* (celebration, dance)

Roth, Gabriel. *Bones.* (dance, release)

————. *Initiation.* (rites of passage)

Serpentine. *Rock the Goddess.* (women's rituals)

Shenandoah, Joanne. *Matriarch.* (women's rituals)

Shulman, Richard. *Ascension Harmonics.* (meditation, healing)

Skanson, Darren Curtis. *Peace, Earth and Guitars.* (relaxation)

Stearns, Michael, and Ron Sunsinger. *Singing Stones.* (release, invoking spirit)

Valley of the Sun. *The Eternal OM.* (meditation)

SUGGESTED READING

Achterberg, Jeanne. *Imagery in Healing: Shamanism and Modern Medicine*. Boston: New Science Library, 1985.

Arrien, Angeles. *The Four-Fold Way*. San Francisco: Harper San Francisco, 1993.

Brener, Anne. *Mourning & Mitzvah: A Guided Journal for Walking the Mourner's Path Through Grief to Healing*. Woodstock, VT: Jewish Lights Publishing, 1993

Bolen, Jean Shinoda, M.D. *Goddesses in Everywoman: A New Psychology of Women*. San Francisco: Harper San Francisco, 1985.

_____. *Gods in Everyman*. New York: Harper & Row, 1989.

Campbell, Joseph. *The Hero with a Thousand Faces*. Princeton, NJ: Bollingen Series, Princeton University Press, 1983.

_____. *The Masks of God*. 4 vols. New York: Viking Press, 1959, 1968.

_____. *The Power of Myth*. New York: Doubleday, 1988.

Cunningham, Scott. *Magical Aromatherapy*. St. Paul, MN: Lewellyn Publications, 1996.

Eagle, Brook Medicine. *Buffalo Woman Comes Singing*. New York: Ballantine Books, 1991.

Gibran, Kahlil: *The Prophet*. New York: Alfred A. Knopf, 1964.

Gimbutas, Marija. *The Language of the Goddess*. San Francisco: Harper & Row, 1990.

Goldstein, Joan, and Manuela Soares. *The Joy Within: A Beginner's Guide to Meditation*. New York: Simon & Schuster, 1990.

Graves, Robert. *New Larousse Encyclopedia of Mythology*. New York: Hamly, 1968.

Harvey, Andrew, and Anne Baring. *The Divine Feminine: Exploring the Feminine Face of God Around the World*. Berkeley, CA: Conari Press, 1996.

Joy, W. Brugh. *Joy's Way*. Los Angeles: J. P. Tarcher, 1979.

Jung, Carl G. *Man and His Symbols*. New York: Dell Publishing, 1968.

Keen, Sam. *Fire in the Belly: On Being a Man*. New York: Bantam, 1991.

Levine, Stephen. *Embracing the Beloved: Relationship As a Path of Awakening*. New York: Doubleday, 1995.

Moore, Robert, and Douglas Gillette. *King, Warrior, Magician, Lover: Rediscovering the Archetypes of the Mature Masculine*. New York: HarperCollins, 1990.

Moore, Thomas. *Education of the Heart*. New York: HarperCollins, 1996.

Northrup, Christiane, M.D. *Women's Bodies, Women's Wisdom: Creating Physical and Emotional Health and Healing*. New York: Bantam Books, 1994.

Phillips, Jan. *Marry Your Muse*. Wheaton, IL: Quest Books, 1997.

St. Claire, Olivia. *Unleashing the Sex Goddess in Every Woman*. New York, Harmony Books, 1996.

Sills, Judith, Ph.D. *A Fine Romance*. New York: Ballantine Books, 1987.

Speller, Jon P., D.D. *Seed Money in Action: Working the Law of Tenfold Return*. New York: Robert Speller & Sons, 1965.

Stone, Merlin. *Ancient Mirrors of Womanhood: Our Goddess and Heroine Heritage*. New York: New Sibylline Books, 1979.

Teish, Luisah. *Carnival of the Spirit*. San Francisco: Harper San Francisco, 1994.

Thich Nhat Hanh. *The Long Road Turns to Joy: A Guide to Walking Meditation*. Berkeley, CA: Parallax Press, 1996.

Tisserand, Robert. *Essential Oil Safety Data Manual*. Brighton, Sussex, England: The Association of Tisserand Aromatherapists, 1985.

Walker, Barbara G. *The Woman's Dictionary of Symbols & Sacred Objects*. Edison, NJ: Castle Books, 1988.

_____. *The Woman's Encyclopedia of Myths and Secrets*. San Francisco: Harper & Row, 1983.

SOURCES

LIFE TREE OILS
3949 Longridge Ave.
Sherman Oaks, CA 91423
Send $2 for catalog:
818-789-2610
essential oils, specialty blends

ENFLEURAGE
321 Bleecker St.
New York, NY 10014
212-691-1610
essential oils, diffusors

STICKS, STONES
AND BONES
111 Christopher St.
New York, NY 10014
212-807-7024
Incense, charcoal, fireproof bowls, crystals, drums, and ritual tools

HANDMADE DRUMS BY
MARK PIXLEY
P.O. Box 1268
Ketchum, Idaho 83340
208-726-3477

PERSONAL ALTARS
Sante-Sacred Spaces
Yoanna Da vinci
325 E. 89th St., Suite 6F
New York, NY 10021
212-737-5342

For information on workshops, audiotapes, and customized ritual kits contact:

BLUE LOTUS PRODUCTIONS
P.O. Box 500
New York, NY 10014
TEL (212) 741-3358
FAX (212) 463-7852
email: britual@aol.com